2,501 Things That Really Piss Me Off

2,501 Things That Really Piss Me Off

A Catalog of Insults and Intrusions That are Sure to Ruin My Day

Being a compendium that also includes annoyances, grievances, vexations, nuisances, affronts, malevolences, mortifications, molestations, provocations, indignities, and humiliations that are really worth griping about.

—◦◦◦—

Assembled by

Herb W. Reich

SKYHORSE PUBLISHING

Skyhorse Publishing books may be purchased in bulk at special discounts for sales promotion, corporate gifts, fund-raising, or educational purposes. Special editions can also be created to specifications. For details, contact the Special Sales Department, Skyhorse Publishing, 307 West 36th Street, 11th Floor, New York, NY 10018 or info@skyhorsepublishing.com.

Skyhorse® and Skyhorse Publishing® are registered trademarks of Skyhorse Publishing, Inc.®, a Delaware corporation.

Visit our website at www.skyhorsepublishing.com.

10 9 8 7 6 5 4 3 2 1

Library of Congress Cataloging-in-Publication Data is available on file.

ISBN: 978-1-61608-572-8

Printed in China

To

Gerri, Mandy, Liza, and Jordyn

The women in my life

None of whom merits inclusion

Contents

"*I'm* mad as hell and *I'm* not going to take it anymore."

—Howard Beale

Preface

*O*ur neighbors outrage us, strangers insult us, unscrupulous entrepreneurs victimize us, our children mock us, government agencies mistreat us, even inanimate objects conspire to screw up our lives; compelling inner voices harass us, the crowd in the agora thwarts us, and irrationality abounds around us. And that is on a good day.

This is a book about anger. And about frustration. It is a catalog of all those things that interfere with the placidity of my life, that make daily living less genial than it could be. It is about man's inhumanity to man—or woman's to woman, if you prefer—no genderism intended.

Friends have counseled me to be more accommodating to the foibles of life, to turn the other cheek, to ignore the bad and dwell on the good, to simply let it all, as they put it, roll off my back.

No way!

The motto on my family crest reads: *Life is too short not to bear a grudge.* And if it is against my nature to seek physical revenge on those who have slighted me, I reserve the right to gripe about them. It is the American way.

Complaining, psychologists assert, is good for the soul. It acts as a relief valve to help dispel the pent-up energy generated by our frustration. If we weren't able to complain, shrinks tell us, we would no doubt exhibit more physical violence and engage more frequently in destructive behavior.

So complaining also serves a social function.

But be aware that most of the things that oppress me are not idiosyncratic. To a large extent we all share them. The reader will be enriched by the realization that the demons that confound him confound the rest of us, as well. This book will demonstrate that misery loves company, and that we are the company that misery loves.

Note that the number in the title is not meant to be taken literally. Like most numbers in the Bible, it is metaphoric—meant to indicate a fairly large quantity. The actual count may be somewhat smaller or somewhat greater. But it is sizeable. Is this a lot to be offended by? Depends on your point of view, your equanimity, your ability to adapt, and your boiling point. A true malcontent will be angered by many fewer, a pious man would likely tolerate many more. Which places me, I suppose, somewhere between malcontentment and piety, neither of which dispositions I would willingly embrace.

Acknowledgments

I would like to offer my thanks to everyone who helped me complete this book. So I shall: Herewith my thanks to everyone who helped me complete this book.

Approaching the final stages of the manuscript (the first time), I realized I had likely overlooked at least a few really flagrant grievances, so I moved outside my narcissistic enterprise to ask some friends if they had anything to add. Their responses, I was pleased to discover, revealed that they were pissed off by much the same as was I. However, they did provide a few notably choice new sources of resentment that I have now included.

I am especially grateful to Frank Schall, Victor Keiser, and Elaine Vogel for sharing their pique with me. Their anger and indignation helped support me in my time of need. I am obliged also, alphabetically, to Roberta Brown, Karen Coffey, Nora and Tito Cohen, Lyle Ecoff, Paul Feiner, David Fischer, Gerry Greenberg, Jennifer Hartig, Steve and Karen Lawless, Ina Reich, Shannon Rosenman, Dr. Dorian Tergis, and my daughter Liza, all of whom aired their bile freely in good spirits. No finer group of malcontents will ever be assembled.

Most authors are careful to affirm that any errors, omissions, or mistatements are theirs alone, absolving all contributors of collusion. Not I. If the reader discovers any of the above-named gaffes, I will gladly share the blame with all of my contributors, consultants, advisers, correspondents, donors, and anyone else who came within twenty feet of the developing manuscript. We can all play a part; it's the democratic way.

Prelude

For openers, I must admit that not all the items reported in this book really piss me off. Some amaze me, some amuse me, some abuse me, some confuse me, but even these can be justified as entries within the scope of the title. And I must further admit that some warrant griping more than others. Some make me seethe with anger, some merely irk me with the stupidity they imply, some just make me wonder about why our species hasn't been better socialized in its millennia on this planet.

The provocation for the present collection occurred one afternoon while browsing through a small book store in London, where I found a little piece of fluff called something like *3,000 Reasons to Be Happy*. (I am fairly certain this wasn't the precise title, but it does accurately represent the tenor of the work.)

It was intermittently moving, joyous, childish, optimistic, simplistic, thankful—but always suffused with a vapor of treacle. It would have served well as an addendum to a Sunday sermon extolling the advantages of living in modern times. Surely, I thought, the world needs a corrective to counterpose this kind of Pollyannish muck.

Yes, there is much around us to celebrate, but the eye of the realist (or the cynic, if you will) observes just as much to outrage. Virtue exists, but so too does iniquity. Goodness is countered by malice, kindness by malevolence, courtesy by churlishness, humanity by barbarity, and so on through an endless catalog of opposing human qualities. Yin, meet yang. Right, meet wrong. Abbott and Costello, meet Frankenstein.

In the service of balancing the scales, I offer this inventory of offenses. Most are time-honored. An anthropologist studying ancient Rome has reportedly found scribbled among the graffiti on the wall of the Colosseum the inscription, *Non illegitimati carborundum,* "Don't let the bastards grind you down." Take heed. Join the dissent. When in Rome do as the Romanians do. Fight back. Get angry. Vent your spleen. Shout it out. Let your voice be heard.

But this roster is not assumed to be exhaustive. Although the present list includes some items suggested by friends, surely you have some of your own pet peeves that have not been mentioned in the inventory that follows. For you, we have left blank pages at the end of the book on which to record your own personal vexations that the present compiler may have omitted. Here is the place to get them off your chest. List them, reread them, and enjoy the catharsis of committing them to paper, where they will become part of the manifest recounting of your grievances. You might even want to submit them to my attention at the publisher's address for inclusion in an ensuing volume, should one comes to pass.

Above all, reflect on the following snippets. Let the bile flow. Rant where necessary. Rave when it seems appropriate. Laugh at the inanities rife in our culture . . . or what passes as. Commit it all to memory; we may ask questions later. And don't forget to buy a few additional copies of this book for your friends . . . who probably wouldn't do the same for you. And that should really piss you off.

Note on the organization: The main body of the book is a random list of those outrages that confront my life. Following are a few topical groupings of related offenses: stupid quotes by politicians, denials of the obvious, deceptive euphemisms, clichés of television, and finally banalities in film.

The Offenders

lawyers

politicians

paparazzi

my cousin Marvin

people who have graduated from assertiveness courses

people who leave the price on a gift

when I find dirty words in my alphabet soup

bait-and-switch practices

the boss's salary

when they make bad movies out of good books

people who don't leash their dogs

yentas

the Macarena

e-mail spam

waiters who ask, "Who ordered the . . . ?"

parents who don't parent

credit cards that arrive in the mail unsolicited

Eurotrash

people who are always late

people who are always early

hackers

nineteen-year-old technomillionaires

people who don't understand me

people who do understand me

repetition

reiteration

redundancy

prolixity

superfluidity

why *brassiere* is singular but *panties* is plural

checks that bounce

tennis balls that don't

when police arrest a mime, they must tell him he has the right
  to remain silent

bad drivers

bad putters

I can never find the inside of my Mobius strip

all day long I've been trying to find out what time it is, and
    everyone gives me a different answer

anything teal

cookies made with lard

talking heads on TV

people who are out to get me

paranoia

that the ancient Greeks never learned to write English so we
    could read them in the original

Venus envy

premature elaboration

when my beer goes flat

when my bacon isn't crisp

accordion players

preachers who dabble in politics

politicians who dabble in preaching

the sink spigot that gurgles unproductively, then suddenly
    hoses out a tsunami wave that floods over the front of my
    trousers

hitting a succession of red traffic lights when I'm late for an
    appointment

nepotism

there is no other word for synonym

trompe l'oeil shower curtains

.com

being hit by lightning

newspaper delivery boys who never miss the roof

PTAs that hold cocktail parties to raise money for stop-student-drinking programs

the picture in my closet is getting really ugly

colorized Marx Brothers films

three-card monte games on the street

doctor's receptionists who think they are working for the Almighty

doctors who think their receptionists are working for the Almighty

the slings and arrows of outrageous fortune

the whips and scorns of time

the oppressor's wrong

the proud man's contumely

the pangs of dispriz'd love

the law's delay

the insolence of office

the spurns that patient merit of the unworthy takes

people who display their learning

politicians who dedicate themselves to making the country safe for hypocrisy

body piercing

sanctimonious political candidates

French poodles with polished nails

French poodles

getting a menu of options when I call 911

Panglossian optimism

pseudointellectual display

obfuscating euphemisms

the tax code

the word phonetic isn't spelled the way it sounds

paper cuts

songwriters who rhyme go with befo'

supercilious head waiters

the annoying music played while I'm waiting on the phone for
    a human voice

the annoying music played in elevators

the annoying music played in my daughter's room

the Psychic Friends Network not being able to predict that
    they were going bankrupt

cutesy TV News anchors

hair loss

memory loss

job loss

sentences that begin, "The thing is . . ."

fortune cookies that lie to me

the weather in Buffalo

psychiatrists haven't discovered one really good new phobia in
    decades

computer prodigies and their megathingies

my shrink reads "War and Peace" while I'm on the couch

the bank pays interest quarterly, but charges interest monthly

my passport picture

I can't figure how Teflon sticks to the pan

borborygmus

my inability to trisect an angle

exhibitionists with nothing to exhibit

diner waitresses who call me "Hon"

the broken E string on my ukulele

Days of Our Lives excludes Saturdays and Sundays

General Hospital doesn't accept insurance assignment

The Guiding Light went out

palm buzzers

lapel flowers that squirt water

plastic dog doo

dribble glasses

whoopee cushions

dribble cushions

whoopee glasses

the infirmity of good taste in modern society

election results are too often determined by which candidate
    spent the most money

lawyers

getting hit in the head by a pelota

dandruff

a turnover on the one-yard line

mirrors that distort my reflection

mirrors that don't distort my reflection

the scurrilous inaccuracies and manufactured controversies in
    supermarket tabloids

I wasn't born rich instead of handsome

I wasn't born handsome

high LDL

the guest room TV that automatically resets to Hotel Channel
    every time it's turned off

melancholia

obtuse angles

obtuse anglers

the word lisp has an "s" in it

reality

hero worship

whiners

people who are more inept than we give them credit for

entropy

telephone solicitations at dinner time

bad toupees

overnight letters that arrive a week later

theatre-goers who understand Ionesco

Sophia Loren has stopped making movies

Tori Spelling hasn't

the salesman who talked me into buying a green plaid suit

the company that made the green plaid suit

the green plaid suit

agita

vulgarity

frivolous lawsuits

the cost of a campaign for election to public office

any bacchanalia to which I have not been invited

being tickled

being tackled

being tarred and feathered

potholes

losing my short-term memory

potholes

unintentionally paying for my dentist's children to go to Ivy
    League colleges

root canal work that extends to graduate school

being groped in a public place
being groped in a private place
undercooked meats in nouveau cuisine
whoever dreamed up blueberry bagels
Lady Gaga's Monster Balls
bad Elvis impersonators
good Elvis impersonators
the equanimity with which we accept mediocrity
the magician who pulls a rabbi out of a hat
making a wrong turn on a pilgrimage
spherical aberration in my shaving mirror
menus with sandwiches named after celebrities
the proliferation of awards dinners
the change of time zones when traveling
psychological analyses of *Gilligan's Island*
potholes
I forgot
not knowing the difference between that and which
not knowing the difference between who and whom
whomever it is which don't know the difference
Godot never showed up
Lefty never showed up
my airplane luggage never showed up
Sheridan Whiteside never left

finding out that the Shadow doesn't know

catheters

when my coupons expire the day before I go shopping

high-fivers

high taxes

high colonics

the accusatory look on Le Penseur

artistic pretension

the incredible wastefulness of the Crusades, especially the
    Children's Crusade

religious fanatics of any kind

our loss of innocence

our loss of civility

people who pontificate

mimes

their team 26, my team 0

the disappearance of spittoons

Chia pets that don't stop growing

lubricity

plangency

anfractuosity

strangury

people who try to impress me with their pretentious vocabu-
    lary

being the company that misery loves

writers who seem to always split an infinitive

our schools no longer teach civics

having a tandem bike and no one to ride it with

traffic gridlock

broken parking meters

the word "monosyllabic" has five syllables

tall, leggy, beautiful blond models who seem to prefer funny-
    looking, dumpy, bald, ignorant guys with bad breath who
    happen to be extremely rich

I'm getting forgetful

potholes

I never had a dog named Toto

I never had anything named Rosebud

I never could name that tune

we don't yet have a medical school degree in proctopsychi-
    atry—for specialists with patients who have their heads up
    their asses

the ephemeral metaphoric vocabularies of art critics and wine
    afficionados

equivocating

pet psychologists

people who act as if they have a monopoly on the truth

people who alter reality to support their point of view

smiley-face balloons

I think, therefore I am not Descartes

plus ça change, plus c'est la même chose

kamikaze pilots wore helmets

drivel

cacophony

parvenus

sycophants

moral turpitude

lawyers

politicians

whenever I switch lanes in traffic, the lane I moved into slows
    down and the one I just left speeds up

we've lost Peanuts

we've lost Calvin & Hobbes

Pauly Shore movies

polka dot lederhosen

hour-long messages on my answering machine that leave no
    space for other callers

Pete Rose has not been elected to the Hall of Fame

there's no longer a distinction between fame and notoriety; it's
    now all just celebrity

naming airplane luggage after Amelia Earhart and expecting it
    to arrive at its destination

not being allowed to play on the Net all day at work
pork barrel legislation, especially when introduced by
    congressmen who loudly proclaim their aversion to high
    taxes and government waste
wine in a box
the people next door
the floor plan of my house was laid out by Maurits Escher
I never saw J. Edgar Hoover in his party frock
the incredibly loud sound of dripping water the morning after
    some serious drinking
the pirates of penance
prerecorded phone solicitations
holding a full house against four of a kind
governmentese
bad news travels at twice the speed of good news
farm subsidies paid for not planting
ignorance
stupidity
bigotry
venality
vice presidents who can't spell "potato"
the outrageous tastelessness that passes as haute couture
Colonel Mustard in the closet with Miss Scarlet
Miss Scarlet in the closet with the candlestick

leaky coffee cups

idolatry

auctioning body parts on e-Bay

the thousand natural shocks that flesh is heir to

child abuse

parent abuse

spousal abuse

police abuse

the popularity of exposed navels

identifying an octopus as a sea animal with eight testicles

Pamper-wearing babies in public pools

road hogs

someone else's flatulence

confusing hype with achievement

cab drivers who don't know how to get from here to there

children's beauty pageants

ominous figures in the night

ominous figures on a P&L

type A personalities

the politicization of the news on the Fox network

chain letters, especially on e-mail

making the same mistake twice

mustard plasters

speed traps

the behavior of some royals

bumper stickers that say, "My child can beat up your honor
    student."

pastrami sandwiches served with mayonnaise

inattentive waiters

crematoria that don't give discounts for burn victims

waiters in a crowded restaurant who ask, not too subtly, "You
    still workin' on that?"

polysemous words

shallow profundity

bee stings

shrapnel

how few stars appear on *Dancing With the Stars*

the government didn't bail me out

Savonarola's execution

when my dentist says, "this won't hurt"

not getting the larger one

the abandon with which universities award unjustified
    honorary degrees

people who oppose abortion but favor the death penalty. (It
    seems not a matter of what, but of when.)

people who oppose the death penalty but favor abortion

Howard Stern's protracted preadolescence

being asked for a midstream sample in a paper cup. And no
    wash and wipes available.

rudeness

missing plane connections

missing train connections

missing connect-the-dot connections

the gravitational density of black holes

the speed of light

existential angst

the traffic on the Grande Corniche

people who respond with "No problem" rather than a
    courteous "You're welcome"

giant squid

the Vatican's castration of so many masterful sculptures

the unhappy fate of Pelleas and Melisande

needlepoint *Bless Our Happy Home* wall hangings

moose-scented incense

your knowing smirk

your smirking knowledge

the time it takes to get to Neptune

profligacy

my inability to tie a timber hitch

"a slim chance" and "a fat chance" mean the same

"flammable" and "inflammable" mean the same

"slow down" and "slow up" mean the same

"wise guy" and "wise man" do not mean the same

noses can run, but feet can smell

the level of civic ignorance in this country: *Newsweek* research
found only 38 percent of citizens were able to pass America's official citizen test

tight shoes

loose morals

gutter balls

tongue studs, eyebrow studs, nipple studs, belly button studs

when the other team kicks a field goal

when my team misses a field goal

predictable plot lines

gilt complex

a film in which not one car is blown up

mosquito bites

Gresham's Law

people who throw garbage out of car windows

political spin doctors

greed

palmetto bugs

bedbugs

I've never been invited to the White House

pom poms

know-it-all columnists

Vanessa Williams was disqualified as Miss America

"batteries are not included"

MSG

when I can't spell antidisistablishmentareanism

when I can't pronounce antidisestablishmentarianism

when the traffic cop who stops me is younger than I am

when my doctor, my dentist, and my attorney are younger than
    I am

when my doctor, my dentist, and my attorney trade magazines
    for the reception room

politicians who don't know when to get off the stage

plane passengers who try to stuff steamer trunks in the over-
    head luggage compartment

dogs who display their friendliness by slobbering all over me

dogs who display their friendliness by humping my leg

shoveling snow

cleaning up leaves in October/November

people who suck their teeth

necrophagia

necromancy

back-slapping salesmen

overnight flights

never winning a Pulitzer Prize

never winning an Oscar

never winning an Emmy

never winning an argument with my wife

tepid coffee

plastic flowers

one of John Keats's finest poems, "On First Looking Into
Chapman's Homer," mistakenly credits Cortez with
discovering the Pacific Ocean (it was Balboa)

garden slugs

grandmothers playing ingénue roles

when a house burns up, it burns down

the volume of junk mail during election seasons

watermelon-flavored bubblegum

cherry-flavored cough medicine

religious zealots at my front door (frequently with pamphlets)

finding advertising flyers under my windshield wiper

triskaidekaphobia

xanthophobia

I don't agree with what you say, but I'll defend my right to not
agree with you

guys who are out of it because their iPods are always plugged
into their ears

all those electronic gadgets I don't understand

insipid post-game interviews with team members

current events commentators with "insightful" post facto
predictions

computer viruses

any viruses

the constant increases in the cost of postage stamps

every time the cost of postage goes up, the postal service goes
   down

ugly neckties

designer neckties

neckties

overpriced utilities

party guests who assay my medicine cabinet

party hosts who have nothing interesting in their medicine
   cabinets

any time a physician tells me he's absolutely sure what my
   symptoms mean, that's when I get a second opinion

stores that double their prices in time for a "one-third off" sale

artificial cream cheese

meretriciousness

age is a high price to pay for maturity

leaky fountain pens

never to have been introduced to Karl Malden

transparent excuses

foolproof excuses proving me foolish

passwords

the need for passwords

salesmen who won't take no for an answer
waitstaff who start removing plates while some at the table are
    still dining
Schopenhauer's idea of life as tragic
Montaigne's inability to know objective truth
Berkeley's belief that material objects are nothing but
    collections of sensations given a common name
philosophers who know everything about everything, but
    nothing else
funny animal videos
drivers who:
    think they own the road
    pick their nose at stop lights
    refuse to move out of the fast lane when I blink them
    park two feet from the curb
    straddle the white line
    tailgate
    drive at me with their bright lights on
    only slow down at stop signs
    speed through intersections on the yellow light
    play their radios at sound pollution levels
    blow their horns instead of learning to drive better
    speed up approaching a red light and then jam on their
        brakes

don't signal before they turn
signal for a left and then turn right
signal for a right and then turn left
signal for a turn and then don't
consume a six-pack before getting behind the wheel
show no road courtesy
cut me off
cut me off, then give me the finger
get behind me and honk the horn the
    second the light turns green
park in spaces reserved for the handicapped
take up two parking spaces with one car
neap tide
anybody that does anything better than I do
bone bruises
sonic teeth cleaning
illiterate late-night television hosts
illiterate early-morning television hosts
the inflated salaries of many CEOs
company executives who steal their company's assets while they
    bankrupt their employees' retirement plans
war
underdone grouse

overdone grouse

grouse

belief in the Herrenvolk

stepping in gum

sunburn

repeatedly landing on "Go to Jail"

not passing GO

not collecting $200

pet pit bulls

schlock radio

interstate highways in Hawaii

newspeak

long-distance phone companies that have several different
    plans, the least costly of which they never voluntarily tell
    you about

used-car salesmen

fruitcakes

phone scams

religious proselytizers

a golf slice

a golf hook

golf

donut-size spare tires

lawyers

politicians

querulousness

soggy vegetables

mediocre sports players who earn multimillion dollars a year

dirty little men who cop a feel on the subway

Paris traffic

three-minute red lights

J'accuse

according to recent polls, over 30 percent of high school
    students don't know who fought in the Civil War

the smell of lamb cooking

people who don't like cats

cats who don't like people

junk

junkies

charities that ask for more the week after you've sent a check

librarians who can't read

books by authors who can't write

candidates for high office who can't think

that the tape will self-destruct in 10 seconds

tick bites

flea bites

barbers who don't listen

barbers who don't shut up

burnt toast

burnt coffee

funny New Year's Eve hats

when birds nest in my beard

when birds nest in my soup

the military-industrial complex

the Oedipus complex

Freudian slips

the weather in Los Angeles

movie sequels

sequels to movie sequels

being run over by a threshing machine

tyrants who rule two-bit nations

getting lost on the road

when a trooper in a patrol car stops me to ask if I know the
    speed limit. Did he forget it?

when the dairy runs out of my favorite ice cream flavor

soggy pizza crust

soggy french fries

soggy beignets

chicken shadow soup

unisex auto showrooms

androgynous hairdos

when the hot water runs out while I'm showering
soap in my eyes
soup on my vest
sap on my car
when the phone rings just as I'm halfway out the door
when the phone rings just as I'm halfway into the tub
when the elevator fills up just before I get on
when I can't think of someone's name
something advertised as "New and improved." Can't be both. If
    it's improved, it's not new. If it's new, there was nothing
    before to be improved.
doctors' handwriting
"quality time"
when a game breaks out in the middle of a hockey fight
smelly cheeses
keyhole peekers
maudlin drunks
the skanky guy with one earring who guards the velvet rope
$600 sneakers
hotel rooms with no windows
hotel rooms with no bathroom
windows that are painted shut
faux dachshunds
Richard Simmons wannabes

getting seasick in the bathtub

outdated milk containers on the market shelf

alcohol-free beer

that the plural of house isn't hice

dirty grout

the errors in my proof of Fermat's last theorem

the smell of week-old mandrake

stock tipsters

meals with too many calories

meals with too few calories

people who don't understand puns

iatrogenic illness

the guy in the elevator whistling a dirge

sound bites in place of news

radio stations that play nothing but Eddie Fisher recordings

radio stations that play nothing but Iggy Pop recordings

hot dog rolls are sold in packages of 8, but hot dogs are sold in
    packages of 6

twenty-three-year-olds writing autobiographies

men who jingle change in their pockets

men who jingle keys in their pockets

men who play with other stuff in their pockets

men who play with their table settings

waiters who introduce themselves

too much vermouth in my martini

when my martini is stirred rather than shaken

Sartre's meaningless existence

canine adornments

persons who lack imagination

nausea

jocular morticians

blowhard politicians who talk a good game but whose votes
     never match their pronouncements

diners who send back the first bottle of wine just to impress
     their companions

people who water their lawn during a drought

the endless string of Viagra jokes

people who say guns don't kill people, people kill people

people who try to cut in front of me in a line

greed TV shows, like *The Price Is Right*

abstruse treatises

obloquies

ineffective theurgy

when the pizza is delivered cold

when the sushi is delivered warm

acerbity

pay-as-you-go morticians

fee-for-service police departments

privatizing government agencies

the doldrums

the Black Death

people who whisper at the movies loud enough for everyone to
hear

disappearance of the kreuzer

obsequious deference

lyricists who can't rhyme two words

getting lost in the London Underground

the doctor telling me I have something (anything) ending in
-osis

the doctor telling me I have something (anything) ending in
-itis

worse yet, the doctor telling me I have something (anything)
ending in –oma

"reality" TV

Rutgers University paying a higher speaking fee to Snooki than
to Nobelist Toni Morrison

forgetting the numbers in the Gettysburg Address

herpes

succubi

incubi

grappa with guava juice

an empty tankard

crepuscular insects

prognathism

jactitation

obscurantism

the F-clef

gaucheness

bogs

acid reflux

quiche pizza

pre-torn jeans

obstructionism

shower curtains printed in shipwrecks

umbrellas that turn inside out in the wind

oyster parfait

roll-on deodorants that stain my shirts

I can't see the difference between red and green

fourteen-dollar movie tickets

ninety-dollar parking tickets

absolute rulers

applications of the Peter Principle

style hounds

fashion shows

ill-fitting clothes

trying to fold a fitted sheet

a cell phone ringing behind me during the critical scene of the
    movie

the randomness of the universe

land mines

singers who mumble directly into the mike

when my shoelace breaks

toothache

rolled-beef sandwiches on cracked-wheat bread

a fart in a crowded elevator

candy wrappers rattling in a movie theater

telephone solicitors who call me by my first name

sitting behind a driver who has only paper money in an
    exact-change lane

mosquitoes on the back nine

shoppers in the supermarket who wait until the last second to
    take out their checkbook

holding a door open for ten people, none of whom says "thank
    you"

parts of California may fall into the Pacific

when the person on the other end of the phone line suddenly
    says: "Hold on a second. My call-waiting line is ringing."

sticky floors in a movie theater

sticky seats in a movie theater

some television personalities who earn millions of dollars a year
    really believe they're worth millions of dollars a year
narcissism
when my chopstick breaks
being kept waiting by my doctor long after the time of my
    appointment
being kept waiting by my dentist long after the time of my
    appointment
being kept waiting by my optometrist long after the time of my
    appointment
being kept waiting by my daughter long after the time of my
    appointment
the maitre d' who welcomes you into the empty restaurant with
    an officious, "Do you have a reservation?"
the moviegoer with odoriferous feet, who takes off his shoes
    before the film begins
kraits
those little tiny frogs that look so cute but can kill you with just
    one touch
successive bogeys
too much people ain't able to put together a literate sentence
the deterioration of the language
falling off a horse
falling off a hearse

forgetting to close the window before a rainstorm

political candidates whose only platform is cutting taxes

dog owners who don't scoop the poop

consecutive days of rain on vacation

when somebody tells me "Don't worry," that's when I start worrying

AIDS viewed as a personal privacy issue rather than a public health problem, unlike any other infectious disease in the past

losing on the last play

losing in overtime

losing

creepy crawly things

fake cheese

oversolicitous snoops

programmed response menus answering my phone calls

waiters who abandon you after delivering your food

breaking my serve

late-night infomercials that promise "financial security." (If these guys know the secret of getting rich, why aren't they applying it rather than hawking it?)

all-guitar bands

air pockets

airheads

par golfers

lawyers who advertise on TV

lawyers

bad breath

offensive body odor

Mercator projections

running out of blue crayon just as I'm about to color in the sky

absorbent rainwear

splinters

no-see-ums

airborne viral diseases

my back pain

my shoulder pain

dangerous microorganisms in my food

hypocondriasis

ice on my windshield

disposable diapers

mornings after

on honeymoon, going to Viagara Falls

a fortune cookie never told me I would total my car

Bach's Piano Sinatra No. 32

Abercrombie & Fitch offering padded bra bikinis for eight-
    year-olds

a fly buzzing around my head, especially at the dinner table

the rip-off we call style, which just makes it possible for
    clothing manufacturers and fashion shops to sell us a new
    wardrobe every year
mairsy doats and dozy doats and liddle lamzy divey
hut sut ralston on the rillerah
the 400 richest Americans have more wealth than the bottom
    150 million combined
Teddy Roosevelt's Rough Riders didn't attack San Juan Hill;
    their famous charge was made on Kettle Hill
a football isn't pigskin, it's cowhide
a baseball isn't horsehide, it's also cowhide
cab drivers who don't pull over to the curb to pick up or drop
    off passengers
people who don't say, "Thank you."
gross-out movies
horseflies
houseflies
dragonflies
twelve-fingered piano players
the disembodied voice that assures me "Your phone call is very
    important to us," after I've been held on a dead line for
    over five minutes
the phone company offering to retry a busy number for only 75
    cents

over-oily soap

soup with too much garlic

soup with too little garlic

squeaky brakes

people who don't hold open the door for the person behind
them when they go through

society offenders who might well be underground, and who
never would be missed!

the pestilential nuisances who write for autographs—

all people who have flabby hands and irritating laughs—

all children who are up on dates, and floor you with 'em flat—

all persons who on shaking hands, shake hands with you like
that—

the idiot who praises, with enthusiastic tone,

all centuries but this, and every country but his own;

apologetic statesmen of a compromising kind,

third persons who spoil tete-a-tetes, and never seem to mind.

(I've got them on the list. They'd none of 'em be missed!)

cruelty to animals

exploitation of animals

cruelty to children

exploitation of children

answering a question with a question

managed-care medicine

receiving ads on my fax machine

seers pointing out their accurate prognostications but ignoring
their mistakes

our inability to control the growth of kudzu

acquittal on a technicality

despotism

Ku Klux Klan marchers

Ku Klux Klan marchers wearing dirty sheets

stand-up comics who couldn't get a laugh without using their
four-letter words

shouting matches

road rage

libertines

cads

debauchees

rakehells

miscreants

reprobates

scalawags

poltroons

cullions

hoodlums

knaves

blackguards

villains

rascals

rogues

scapegraces

scoundrels

scamps

rapscallions

ne'er-do-wells

the variety of bad guys in older novels

treachery

depravity

the expanding universe

when my computer crashes

playing second fiddle

stubbing my toe

I don't understand why sheep don't shrink when it rains

defense contractors who bill the government $600 for a
    hammer

petulant children

petulant adults

habitual liars

gypsy moths

ragweed

Ronald Dumsfeld hasn't yet been indicted for prescribing
     torture of prisoners while he was Secretary of Defense,
     even though prosecution was requested by the UN
     Commission on Human Rights
the smell of my neighbors' okapi
the smell of my neighbors
my neighbors
my brother-in-law Rocco
the unavailability of a really good egg cream
people who name their car
tobacco company PR men who still claim that nicotine is not
     addictive
hypocrisy
more Americans know the name of at least one judge on
     American Idol than on the Supreme Court
uninformed opinion
racists
political party partisans posing as newscasters
misinformed political spinmeisters
hot-rodders
opera karaoke
the French thinking they invented cooking
cholesterol count over 300

bankers who rail against entitlement programs after collecting
 hundreds of millions from the government
underwear that creeps up
when I can't remember the password
the amateurish acting in porn films
Cleopatra wasn't Egyptian
St. Patrick wasn't Irish
Nick Kenny never made poet laureate
I can't see Russia from my front porch
I can't see Russia from my back porch
I can't see my back porch from my front porch
anorexic fashion models
my second wife's third husband
kids no longer just go out to play
when I trip on backsy foursies
jihadists
when the caravansary loses my reservation
the social pressure to sport a new wardrobe every year
we call them newscasters while the British, more accurately, call
 them news readers
Toyota gas pedals that go into business for themselves
I still can't find a buyer for my 1958 Edsel
the loss of privacy
we won't have any new Capra films

my congressman has better medical coverage than I have
the shrinking value of the dollar
the Caribbean end of the Panama Canal is farther west than
 the Pacific end
we haven't had a Triple Crown winner since 1978
Gretzky didn't leave any records for another hockey player to
 achieve
Vatican City doesn't have one kosher deli
somebody from New Orleans who has no rhythm
celebrities who are celebrities for no other accomplishment
 than being celebrities
having 15 when the dealer shows a picture
another form of child abuse—cutesy training
swatting lies with a fungo bat
people who use handheld phones while driving
people who text while driving
people who read a newspaper while driving
drunk drivers
drunk putters
drunk drivers who have kids in the car
when the motherboard is fried
when the modem disconnects
not finding the right power cord
cat puke

cat poop on the floor around the litter box

cat pee under the litter box

movie reviews that give away the ending of mystery films

people who dress their kids like prostitots

when cling wrap doesn't

cars that cost more than a house

mail spam

baseless lawsuits

face tattoos on women

calling Kenny G's music jazz

parents who allow their tots to run free in supermarkets

in Shakespeare's "Antony and Cleopatra" (II, 5), Cleo asks to
     play billiards, but the game wasn't to be invented until the
     fourteenth century

in Shakespeare's "Julius Caesar" (II, 1), Brutus hears a clock
     strike the hour, but history dates the earliest known such
     mechanism from early-eighth-century China

smoking electrical outlets

when the microwave melts my dishes

six-week-old Limburger cheese

fender benders

posing on the red carpet

the crap they put on E! TV channel

Craig Ferguson isn't on the air 24/7

political campaigning has become a blood sport

an expurgated "Henny Penny"

a Botox non-smile

bird poop through my car's sun roof

I've never seen Heidi Montag's real face

Joan Rivers bringing a new low to American culture with the
     line, "Who are you wearing?"

cigarettes used to taste so good

poverty

extreme wealth

the incomprehensibility of tax return instructions

war films that sanitize battle scenes

auto recalls

The Girls Next Door don't live next door

the paucity of airline seats allotted to frequent flyer miles

"y'know...."

customer reps who say "Youse"

the word "I" has been replaced by "Ah" in pop music

politicians more concerned with the image of their party than
     the needs of the country

people carrying on loud cell phone conversations in public
     places

auto mechanics who replace parts that don't need replacement

kickbacks

when the supermarket puts a $1.50 item on "special sale 3 for
$5.00"

when I miss a two-foot putt

a 7–10 split

little dogs with big attitudes

riptides

exorbitant bonuses to bankers who caused the financial
meltdown

when California smog gets so heavy UCLA becomes U don't
CLA

the double 0 on roulette wheels

the network genius who decided to put Jay Leno in a prime-
time TV show

mice in my pantry

when my nuts and my bolts don't match

hair pomade

bathroom deodorant that smells like potted meat

potted meat that smells like bathroom deodorant

bail jumpers

Bernie Madoff with my money

all the trees we're wasting publishing so-called exposé magazines

I can never find the right place for 8s in my Sudoku

SRO on my commuter train

SRO in my bathroom

boxcars

four-day-old coffee

wearing one black sock and one blue sock . . . and I realize I
    have another pair just like that at home

Angelina Jolie won't adopt me

Babe Ruth couldn't sink a basket from the foul line

pucks aren't made in Day-Glo colors

when the phone company gives me a window of 1:00 to 5:00
    for repair and shows up at 4:59

anyone who's full of himself, or herself, as the case may be

I've never heard anyone play jazz musical saw

apathy

torpidity

appliances that fail the day after their warranty expires

swine flu

blankets with sleeves

governors visiting their girlfriends in Argentina. Don't we have
    enough broads here in the US?

tea parties

we no longer have a Walter Kronkite to report unbiased news

women convinced to believe that diamonds show love

everything I buy is made in China

the cost of life-saving drugs

we buy oil from countries committed to destroying us

drops in the DJI

the door to my bathroom doesn't lock

Toys for Sots

a leaky roof

unemployment

E-coli in my hamburger

peach cannelloni

senators caught carousing in DC fountains with strippers

senators caught carousing in DC fountains with other senators

congressmen caught in the cloakroom with a page

congressmen caught with an underage hooker

those additions congressmen make to bills after they've been
    voted on

"trust me"

ad hominem political advertising

the kid ringing my bell on Halloween who has a chauffeured
    car waiting at the curb

I can't get three cherries on the one-arm bandit

genocide in Darfur

hungry children

hungry adults

phone calls that begin, "Your home insurance is about to expire
    ..."
supermarket checkout clerks who can't subtract $1.87 from
    $2.00
auto repair shops that fix things not broken
the arrogance of politicians
inherited megawealth
zigging when I should have zagged
aroma wasn't built in a day
Doris wasn't built in a Day
Jack Nicholson cast as Little Lord Fauntleroy
Henny Penny, the sky is falling
"sitcom" is a word translated from the Assyrian
you can't choose your face, but you can pick your nose
waiters who don't know their place settings
fun is fun, and games are games, but Wednesday still comes
    after Tuesday
the sound of my neighbor's leaf blower at 7:00 o'clock on a
    Saturday morning
the sound of my neighbor's lawn mower at 7:30 on a Sunday
    morning
the sound of my neighbor
when my red wine turns white
when my two cents plain goes flat

when my rowboat starts taking on water

the butcher weighing my meat is charging me for his thumb

marathoners who do part of their route on the subway

the outrageous interest rate on credit cards

Funniest Home Videos finding humor in people getting hurt

my jodhpurs make me look like my thigh has a goiter

our local cemetery is called an interment camp

there are no collectible polo player cards

my wife snores in the key of A-flat

too many people say sex when they mean gender, but no one
    says gender when they mean sex

"ough" can be pronounced at least eight different ways

nobody uses the word "whence" anymore

carolers on Arbor Day Eve

being stylish just to display that you can afford to be

assault weapons

people who cheat at Bingo

whatever happened to peak lapels?

I feel naked without my spats

I'm expected to buy certain hardware because it's advertised by
    big boobs

my potato soup has a leek in it

"This will hurt me more than it hurts you."

trying to fit a three-prong electrical plug into s two-hole socket

what 4-inch heels do to a woman's feet
ungracious hosts
ungracious guests
I can't find decaffeinated gin
my belt size, 32 inches two years ago, is now 42 inches
measuring my commuting time in light-years
Paris is full of Parisians
I can't get succotash in lemon flavor
cluster bombs
high schools graduating kids who haven't learned to read
finding a Purple Heart medal in a pawn shop
when the previous guest in my hotel room set the alarm for
    6:00 AM and didn't turn it off when he left
clogged downspouts
paint peeling off my ceiling
birthdays that end in "0"
being burned at the stake
being burned at the steak
being drawn and quartered
"the official (anything) of the New York Yankees"
based on where they play, the New York Giants should be
    called the New Jersey Giants
trichinosis
M1N1

'twas brillig

UFOs

I have so much humility, I'm frequently humiliated

nosy neighbors

nosy coworkers

"Honk if you . . ."

"May I see your driver's license and registration?"

the Puritans, who came to America to escape religious intolerance, refusing to permit religious freedom for others in
their colonies

the eighteenth amendment to the Constitution did not
prohibit drinking or possessing alcohol, only manufac-
turing or selling it

the jury finding Lizzie Borden innocent of killing her mother
and father

plum pudding has no plums in it

Dr. Seuss wasn't a real doctor

two wrongs don't make a right, but three rights do make a left

untended car alarms that seem to go on interminably

noogies

Ed Wood never won an Oscar

Tony Soprano was really a baritone

Dick Cheney hasn't invited me to go hunting with him

West 4th Street crosses West 10th Street in New York City's
    Greenwich Village
can't get a decent ham sandwich anywhere in Haifa
can't get a hamburger anywhere in Kathmandu
I'm paying more taxes than the General Electric Company
Cal Ripken Jr. retiring
Congress funding weapons systems the military doesn't want
love goes out the door when distrust comes innuendo
where there's a will there are heirs
Survivor: Coney Island
handlebar mustaches
not one financial officer who was responsible for the bank
    failure has been indicted
gory movies
bands in which the drummer carries the melody
slot machines that don't pay off
drawing a 2 when doubling down with a 5 and a 6
"No Parking" signs
icing the puck
I don't want a Will; I'm writing a Won't
my broker has a yacht; I don't even have a dinghy
short-circuits
when the auto mechanic gives me an estimate of $60 and later a
    bill for $300

the arrogance of power

the power of arrogance

New York City's ex-police commissioner pleading guilty to several federal crimes

members of Congress who loudly advocate deficit reduction through cutting social programs, never include trimming their own retirement perks or medical coverage

when Sam doesn't play it again

when Simon doesn't say

millionaires able to outspend competitors and buy political office

sports are no longer games; they're now all about the numbers

politicians

lawyers

politicians who are lawyers

"The fact of the matter is . . ." is usually followed by a lie or a massive exaggeration

when I get stuck in the HOV lane behind a little old lady doing 5 miles per hour and in front of an impatient teenage hot-rodder with a heavy horn hand

when I discover that my $130 restaurant check covers $40 for the food and the other $90 for the artistic presentation

shells on a half clam

$a^2 + b^2$ never $= g^2$

bankers

arbitrageurs

financial derivatives

bankers who deal in derivatives

women spending hours putting on makeup just to look natural

the doe who went into the forest to pick up a couple of bucks

the buck who was out just to make some doe

US education gets a failing grade: our students are twenty-sixth
    in the world in math proficiency and eleventh in the world
    in reading proficiency

idiotic courses given at some colleges, like "Zombies in Popular
    Media" at Columbia College in Chicago and "The
    American Vacation" at the University of Iowa. This is
    education?

finding refuse dropped next to an empty garbage can

appliances left along the side of the road or in the woods

restaurants with no noise damping

neighbors with leaf blowers moving leaves from their yard to
    mine

interruptions when I'm speaking

using public roads for drag racing

chain e-mails

driving directions that end with "You can't miss it." (Yes you can, and usually do).

charities that try to solicit guilt contributions by showing pictures of disheveled old people or children with physical deformities

congressmen who are more interested in embarrassing the opposition party than in attending to the needs of the nation

downtime

calling an American company for technical advice and getting connected to somewhere in Asia

people no longer get angry at injustice

French sauces that hide the poor quality of the ingredients

Budapest is really two cities

even a dog in Hong Kong understands more Chinese than I do

my blood thinner is working better on my hair than on my blood

"bald is beautiful"

I just flew in from the produce department, and are my yams tired

a man, a plan, a canal—Suez

black hair with blond roots

everybody talks about the Constitution, but nobody knows what it says

The Offenders

memoirists with creative memories

misogyny

when the gas station jockey puts gas in my car and fails to
    replace the fuel cap

nobody cares anymore what Vanna is wearing

reminiscing just isn't what it used to be

the problem with doing nothing, is you can't tell when you've
    finished

when the guy in front of me on line orders a double cheese-
    burger, extra large fries . . . and a diet coke

fixed sumo bouts

my short-term memory remembers things that my long-term
    memory has forgotten

potholes

drivers who stop in the middle of the street to ask directions
    when there is plenty of room at the curb

there's no longer any distinction between singers and sideshow
    performers

dilettantes

libidinal thoughts during an opera performance

no, Meredith, that isn't my final answer

Oprah is off the air

Wendy Williams isn't

when I have to think of something nice to say about my
    neighbor's ugly newborn
fall back, spring ahead
when the core threatens meltdown
Ben's mother never told him to go fly a kite
being energy-dependent on people who want to kill us
dinner at 4:30 PM in Miami
those who can, do; those who can't, take Viagara
I can't remember the number to dial when I want to reach 911
tenure
waiters who massage their hemorrhoids while bringing my
    food
people who high-five everything
people for whom everything is "awesome"
baby really does need a new pair of shoes
the unbearable suspense in episodes of *The Girls Next Door*
there's no TV show called *WOMANswers*
having the best senators that money can buy
playing politics with government
Dubya's Bush-league administration
gas guzzlers
palming Zs when playing Scrabble

people who have their children record a "cute" message on their
     answering machine
any offer that "expires in two hours"
any phone calls that begins, "Congratulations. You've been
     selected. . . ."
just 'cause they have hard hats doesn't necessarily mean they
     don't have soft hearts
you can't get there from here
when my egg foo yung has too little egg, too little yung, and
     too much foo
when my kartoffel is offal
when I can't take my alligator bag on the plane because they
     don't allow carrion luggage
my call for technical advice ends up in India or the Philippines
the nurse who asks, "How are we feeling today?"— We???
when my house gets TP'd
running out of TP before I finish covering my neighbor's house
the little things living under my sink
starched handkerchiefs
toilet tissue with funny sayings on it
having to stand in the subway
there is no three-dollar bill

the blond model who lives next door never hits on me

Grady Sutton never won an Oscar

calling two men an odd couple. Shouldn't it be an even couple?

I can't find PJs with bell bottoms

Gallia in tres partes divisa est

we never hear of the eighth dwarf named Emily

doglegs

Jim Henson eating frog legs

a leaky sink

the odor of asparagus urine

plastics that won't disintegrate

penis enhancers (play the cards you were dealt)

the size of the Swiss navy

when the elastic wears out on my anklets

trying to understand calculus

Cantor's multiple infinities

Monday mornings

the cost of college tuition

counting out my life in coffee spoons

poetry that doesn't scan

soybean-based schnitzel

Ronald Reagan wasn't elected friend of the president

the Botswana hockey league

a deviated septum

riders to insurance policies in tiny type

government regulators who don't regulate

my aunt has a bushier moustache than I do

my cat wants a raise

hawkers selling 8-tracks on street corners

I can't get my mouth around a pastrami sandwich at the Stage
    Deli

twenty-five-room apartments

Freud never went home for Friday night dinner with the family

avoiding Burger King during Lent

root beer with no fizz

eight is not enough

salary and salami are related etymologically

Anna wasn't the king of Siam

a brake job that costs more than a nose job

inflatable boobs

anybody who is always texting

unselected job applicants who get no courtesy feedback that
    the position has been filled

the mess in Albany

the mess in Washington

the mess in my dining room

bad haircuts

bad grammar

shingles

a flooded basement

a flooded attic

when the parachute doesn't open

twelve seats in a row on an airplane

when one sleeve on my shirt is longer than the other

a paper kilt

newspaper ink rubbing onto my fingers

global warming

the morons in government who deny global warming is
   occurring

ideologues

"What's good for General Motors is good for America"

beauty contest losers running for high office

che sera, Sarah

Chelsea Handler isn't on a real TV station

Jessica doesn't appear on TV with the rest of the Simpsons

Glenn Beck's apocalyptic conspiracy theories

ED isn't a talking horse

self-important celebrities

incest

inaccuracy

inanity

inclemency

incommodiousness

incompetence

inconsiderateness

indelicacy

indifference

indigence

indiscretion

inefficiency

ineptitude

inequality

inequity

infamy

infanticide

infelicity

infidelity

inflexibility

ingratitude

inhumanity

iniquity

injuriousness

insalubrity

insensibility

insensitivity

insidiousness

insincerity

insipidity

insipience

insolence

intimidation

intolerance

intractability

intransigence

intrusiveness

invidiousness

incontinence

finding puddles of soda on my theater seat

finding gum on my airplane seat

when the airplanes shot that poor monkey off the Empire State
    Building

Mickey Rooney always had his uncle's Hippodrome to put on
    his newest show

acid rain

writers who can't spell

newspaper reporters who can't spell

newspaper reporters who can't write

holders of high office who can't think

television yentas posing as show business reporters

sham Haiku poems of nineteen syllables

the road to good intentions is paved with Hell

the super ego in conflict with the superego

when I pick all six Lotto numbers correctly . . . the week before
they hit

baseball players charging fans for their autographs

termite damage

McDonld's Lenten special

Zydeco music played on a zither

discovering that the emperor has no clothes

receiving a telegram that says: "Start worrying, letter follows."

pop psychology

candy for kids packaged in crack vials

when a candidate for major office, having had three wives, and
cheating on two of them, runs on a *preserve the family*
platform

guys who have their jeans pressed

a hangnail

smog

when my accountant can't find enough deductions at tax time

getting hit with a puck at a hockey game

getting hit with a puck at a basketball game

getting hit with a puck in my living room

variable exchange rates when traveling abroad

maniacal looks from strangers on the street

friends telling me I'm paranoid after describing the maniacal
    looks I'm getting from strangers on the street
insurance companies that find ways not to pay valid claims on
    policies
The Beach Boys are no longer boys
the proportion of air time allowed for television commercials
TV commercials broadcast at higher volume than the show
    they are on
the scarcity of public toilets
John Stuart Mill's pursuit of pleasure
wigs that look like they were cut from wall-to-wall carpeting
Galileo removing the earth from the center of the solar system
lawyers
politicians
jazz played on a bagpipe
people who never get pissed off about anything
air pollution
water pollution
ground pollution
people pollution from parents with more kids than fingers
"lifetime" bulbs that last only until the end of the week
warthog tusks
social security seen as middle-class welfare
coffee you have to cut with a knife and eat with a fork

the Tea Party doesn't serve cookies

my mother using my stickball bat as a broom handle

they don't deliver milk to my porch anymore

I could never hit three sewers

my brother's name is Rover, my dog is Irving

the waiter bringing my appetizer, my entrée, and my dessert all
    at once

the guy in front of me in the theater who loudly tells his
    companion how the movie ends

Galli-Circi couldn't scat

grandpa hitting on my girlfriend

my girlfriend passing her number to grandpa

moth holes in my front fender

anything I say may be written down and used against me

Charlie Sheen's irrational moments

whistling in the dark

the microwave tower being built in my vegetable patch

sports fans who paint their bodies

the porn shop won't give me anything for my old silver coffee
    pot

I found a way to keep my hair—in a cigar box

Elizabeth was not my taylor

Rhett was not my butler

Marion was not my maid

when Ilsa leaves Rick at the airport and flies out of Casablanca
with Victor Laszlo

when my pinball machine tilts

"The Protocols of the Elders of Zion"

singers no longer need vocal coaches, now only marketing
managers

the negligence of the US Post Office, which issued a Statue of
Liberty stamp using not the image of Lady Liberty in New
York harbor, but rather of an ersatz statue in front of a Las
Vegas hotel

the inflated costs of a funeral

American business moving jobs offshore

losing my ball on a dogleg

wondering if cowboys in Europe wear thirty-eight-liter hats

I don't know if British homeowners have a backmeter behind
their house?

when the washing machine yields an odd number of socks

travel for too many is just another occasion for shopping,
rather than learning something about other people and
other places

rectal thermometers

One Life to Live is no longer alive

All My Children is (are?) dead

when the *New York Times* started using product names in its
crossword puzzles

one man's meat is another man's poisson

all's fair in love and professional wrestling

the knowledge that nothing exceeds like excess

hypothermia

Wayne Gretsky, John Elway, and Michael Jordan all retired the
same year

I went to the flea market and didn't buy one flea

I can't play Chinese checkers since I lost my marbles

bills payable on the 16th that arrive on the 17th

pseudo-French restaurants that call themselves Chez Some-
thingorother

I will eat French food in a restaurant called A Taste of France,
and Italian food in A Taste of Italy, but not Hellenic food
in A Taste of Greece

texting has replaced reading by young adults

Shiites and Sunnis trying to kill each other

CCCP meant USSR

whenever I misplace something, it always turns up in the last
place I look

birthers

girl singers who display the most skin usually have the least
talent

the idiocy of the *Guinness Book of Records*, which acknowledges
such dubious achievements as most toilets seats broken by
a skull in one minute, or balancing the most beer kegs on
one's head

Spike Jones was not ever invited to play Carnegie Hall

Murphy Brown never won a Pulitzer

the attitude of entitlement displayed by some starlets and
sports figures

Donald Trump posing as a financial savior, despite his having
filed for corporate bankruptcy four times

artificially enlarged body parts

Congress won't cut subsidies to the big oil companies even
though the companies keep showing ever-increasing profits

owner Frank McCourt driving the L.A. Dodgers (in the
distant past, the Brooklyn Dodgers, the beloved Bums, was
my home team) into bankruptcy

page 6 of the *New York Post*

Rupert Murdoch, called "the great vampire of media corruption" by one columnist, plumbing a new low standard for
journalism

the devaluation of the penny

people who use their voice mail to avoid answering the phone

trousers that are cut bowlegged

chicken soup without dill

onion soup without onions

when I don't take my umbrella, and it rains

when I do take my umbrella, and it doesn't rain

warts

the "me-first" generation

blabbermouths

cloning mosquitoes

loud-mouthed blockheads who are ostentatious about their
   stupidity

lying to oneself

lying to me

shoes that pinch

bosses that pinch

waiters that pinch

watery punch

my paunch

raisins in my meatloaf

ramson salad

rapaciousness

any contretemps

melting of the polar cap

the number of candles on my birthday cake

never having attended a Florence Foster Jenkins recital

Ebbets Field is gone

sinkholes

cockroaches

the bombing of Dresden

a coup d'état

older drivers

younger drivers

recidivists

people who give unsolicited advice

impoliteness

being allergic to Shetland wool

keeping up with the Joneses

that weird image I see in the mirror

people who cheat at go-fish

the E-flat tambourine

door-to-door salesmen, especially when I'm trying to nap

Chirico images on packaged products

sponge dice hanging from rear-view mirrors

mystery novels in which the butler did it

mystery novels in which the butler didn't do it . . . but you
    thought he did

travelogues about the Constantinople sewer system

heartburn

chocolate-covered sardines

salmonella turning up all over the place

laces without aglets

dull razor blades

dental caries

people who always have tomato stains in their clothing after
    eating pizza

when the person before me didn't flush the toilet

when giraffes and hippopotami can't live together

having to buy it just because I broke it

being behind a novice air traveler who doesn't know she can't
    wear a pound of jewelry through the metal detector

landing on Park Place after someone else has built a hotel there

people who have never been to Bruges

finishing a 600-piece jigsaw puzzle to find the last piece missing

people who hire decorators to define their own living space

dolts who think Platonic Ideal is a rock group

"Don't call us; we'll call you."

hair shirts

people who claim to understand "Finnegans Wake"

when a pawn takes my king

when a pawn takes my pawn

astrological divination

people who see everything as either black or white

hydroplaning on a curvy road

when one leg on my trousers is longer than the other

the plumber never calling back

a flat tire in the rain

when that raisin on my rice pudding walks away

moo shu with grapes

The Birth of Venus reproduced in paint-by-numbers

day-old guano

chauvinism

finding my fender dented in the parking lot

a rowboat without oars

the way my clothes shrink every year

dirty Ingveonic basketball ditties

starting a new book and finding the dirty parts highlighted

when my highlighter runs out of ink

broccoli-flavored toothpaste

smokers who foul the area by dropping their cigarette butts all
     over the place

anyone with a marked propensity for atavism

the disparity between the idealism of the German philosophers
     and the brutality of the German Nazis

the occult symbolism of Yeats's early poetry

the inherent egotism in Nietzsche's "will to power"

Heidegger's exploration of Nothing

Hegel's admiration for regulation and the order of intense
    government control
sophomoric pretension
ochlocracy
persiflage
rumors that the Empire State Building is that way about the
    Holland Tunnel
when I'm in a public john and the guy in the next cubicle asks
    if I have change for a ten
"smile" buttons
the muscleman who kicked sand in my face at the beach
the service station that has an adjacent restaurant and a sign
    that reads, "Eat here, get gas."
IRS phone agents who give you incorrect advice
I hardly ever see a Good Humor truck anymore
a repair for a bent fender that costs as much as the original car
a bacon and tomato sandwich without lettuce
a bacon and lettuce sandwich without tomato
a tomato and lettuce sandwich without much taste
General Tso's flanken
accommodations on the orlop deck
tour guides who get me lost
I never pick the right card in three-card monte
lumpy guacamole

deconstructing The Three Little Pigs

hairy glabellae

querulous relatives who drop by for the weekend

when the toilet tissue dispenser is empty

when the laundry starches my shorts

pomposity

fustian bombast

uncomfortable chairs

know-it-alls

people who hallucinate

exaggerated fish stories

there's no state quarter for Tijuana

the pointlessness of the Kardashians

wart implants

going over Niagara Falls in a barrel smelling of pickles

frozen wattles

polar bears becoming extinct

assignment to the ducking stool

homes that display not a single book

homes where books are chosen with covers to match the decor

spoiled children

spoiled food

inconsiderate smokers

cloning pit bulls

lawyers who own their own ambulances

backgammon hustlers

lycanthropes

people who never vote

people who never read a newspaper

people who never read a newspaper but do vote

people who don't vote, but loudly lament the inequities of the
    political system

cockfights

gansta rap

reckless skateboarders

"Last round, gentlemen."

feckless repairmen

advertising on the outside of taxis

advertising on the inside of taxis

wine snobs

streakers

mooners

Moonies

armadillos that talk back

hostile takeovers

fish cakes

"going out of business" stores

social promotion in public school

loose teeth

"you guys"

endless menus in some diners

ingrown toenails

having to go all the way to London to see Buckingham Palace

unqualified school bus drivers

government by acronym

people who deface road signs

abdominal cramps

jellyfish

celebtocracy

antediluvian thinking

beauty contest talent segments

celebrating Washington's and Lincoln's birth on the same
    day—which is usually neither's birthdate

we're off the gold standard

squeaky bedroom floorboards

orange-flavored grout

Sisyphean single-mindedness

celebrities who behave as though they've begun to believe their
    own publicity releases

when the elevator breaks down halfway up the Eiffel Tower

Jerry Springer television, with its induced violence

doggerel

as per Mark Twain, the annoyance of a good example

the dishonesty of hyperbole

the realization of how little we know

the price of tickets to Broadway shows

service people indirectly asking for a tip, like the envelope

    inscribed *thank you* that comes with my daily newspaper

false modesty

making the same mistake thrice

pride

covetousness

lechery

anger

gluttony

envy

sloth

the scarcity of heroes in modern society

the junk that frequently passes for fine art

concerts that sell out to ticket speculators (scalpers)

ticket scalpers (speculators)

Judd Nelson is not related to Ozzie and Harriet

gravy stains on my new shirt

gravy stains on my new tie

gravy stains on my new jacket

my sloppy eating habits

gravy that stains

meatless Fridays

fruitless Saturdays

godless Sundays

cabs that don't stop for me on rainy nights

I can never fit tab A into slot B

bent paperclips

jammed staplers

pencils with used-up erasers

pencils with dried-out erasers

not having the right change when I park at a meter

showing movies to focus groups to decide how they should end

weeds growing in the trunk of my car

the ping in my engine

having ping without pong

hocus without pocus

Huey without Louie or Dewey

when I've fallen down and I can't get up

any living thing with more than four legs

finishing second

finishing last

gossip, particularly if I don't know the gossipee

it's been a long time since I've seen a really big shoo
being seated behind a pillar
being seated behind a pillow
frozen wheel nuts
runny scrambled eggs
radioactive crepes
college degrees through the mail
bats in the attic
negative campaigning, by the opposition
not having fingerprints
not casting a shadow
the toast to accompany my lunch never showed up
cannibals won't eat standup comics because they taste funny
unctuous hotel desk clerks
unctuous politicians
unctuousness in general
saddle shoes worn with clocked socks
ties that light up in the dark and say, "Kiss me, baby"
edible yarmulkas
social climbers
stage mothers
stage drivers
human sacrifice
animal sacrifice

getting lost on Wistful Vista

my apartment looks like Fibber McGee's closet

naming Charlie Sheen the designated hitter-oner

corrupt cops

corrupt politicians

teachers who read at the second-grade level

"experts" who replace my ignorance with misinformation

T&A TV

immaculate deception

any film that has more than two car crashes

orange-flavored spackling

so much TV is offal

throwing a can of paint at a canvas and calling it art

the paucity of buskers outside New York theaters

European toilet paper made from shirt cardboard

European store bags made from toilet paper

the loss of my joie de vivre

my large collection of 9-track cartridges

charities that spend 60 percent of their receipts on solicitation

charities that spend the other 40 percent on management
    salaries

bouncers at kiddie amusement parks

when my bumper car doesn't bump

scraping my knuckles
never knowing if a word is misspelled in the dictionary
men who spit like a quarter
American companies promoting contaminated products in
    Third World countries
nobody writes with a quill pen anymore
the new bare-it-all haute coutour
there's no ham in hamburger, no egg in eggplant, and neither
    pine nor apple in pineapple
by the time I get my new computer set up, it's out of date
fifteen minutes of fame now lasts a season of reality TV shows
when my bank loses a cancelled check, then bills me $25 for a
    photocopied replacement
grandiosity
megalomania
ego-centricism
lawyers
politicians
when the clothing salesman steers me to the portly department
the implications of the uncertainty principle
left-handed threads
tennis elbow
housemaid's knee

Achilles' heel

the impossibility of getting anything done while keeping your
    nose to the grindstone, your ear to the ground, and your
    shoulder to the wheel

shaving cuts

when the mortise and tenon don't match

precocious children

Moe and Curly ganging up on Larry

Moe and Larry ganging up on Curly

Larry and Curly ganging up on Moe

when the Customer Service desk announces it will handle only
    seven more problems, and I'm eighth in line

standup comedy used to be clever, now it's too often just
    scatological or smutty

I need a fifteen-million-dollar Lotto win just to break even

mal de tête

mal de mer

mal de chemin de fer

complacency

"Been there; done that."

ghosts

specters

apparitions

promoting an abbreviated twelve-step program in five steps for
    those maladjusted who don't have the time
when it rains on my parade
when I run out of postage stamps
when the bread grows mold
high-pressure salesmen screaming at me on TV
phone calls from boiler room operators
a leaky oil pan
designer coffees
meatless hot dogs
inconsiderate motorcycle jockeys
pizzerias that don't deliver
with all the practicing they do, lawyers should be better at their
    job
when my friends run out of single-malt scotch
having to adjust my clock twice a year to accommodate
    daylight savings time
the desecration of the Venus de Milo
odoriferous sneakers
arms dealers
crack dealers
double dealers
blackjack dealers who won't provide a five when I ask for it

the exponential growth of my school taxes

the exponential growth of my waistline

square bagels

being scorned for not joining the wave at a baseball game

the limited repertoire of sport-stadium organists

the ever-increasing length of the work week

the ever-decreasing size of airplane seats

not getting a seat on the commuter train

pollen in hay fever season

running out of gas

that the Battle of Bunker Hill was actually fought on Breed's
    Hill

interference on my TV screen during my favorite show

the enmity between Gilbert and Sullivan

I don't know one Andrew Lloyd Weber tune I can hum

I can never outthink Sherlock Holmes

the self-deceptive arrogance of the Titanic designers

product liability lawyers who, to quote John Grisham in *The
    Runaway Jury*, plot ways to "mine the mother lode of
    American torts"

the NHL seems unable—or unwilling—to curb players'
    fighting during games

I never saw The Crazy Gang on stage

varicose veins

people who explain it all away with, "If it's not one thing, it's
    your mother."

the Lotto machine never selects the right numbers

discovering that the Omega watch I bought in the stadium
    parking lot is a rip-off

the legal system in which an attorney's role is advocacy rather
    than justice

when my boat springs a leak

taking the road everyone else has traveled

not being the prettiest one at the ball

people who don't believe wrestling is a real sport

what parking lot attendants do to my car

political assassination

character assassination

impropriety

CD wrappings that defy me to open them

auto mechanics who can't find the carburetor

road repairs scheduled during rush hour

cat-scratch fever

neo-Nazism

never filling an inside straight

the bad rap that history has given to Capt. William Kidd, really
    a privateer, not a pirate

hip hop music in the twelve-tone scale

the disappearance of the "I cash clothes" man

unwarranted charges that appear on my monthly credit card
    statement

all ten plagues: blood, frogs, vermin, wild beasts, murrain, boils,
    hail, locusts, darkness, and smiting of the firstborn

I don't know what "murrain" is anyway

a gallon of bottled water costs more than a gallon of gasoline

our loss of pride in a job well done

our loss of common courtesy

that we haven't learned from Ozymandias

too few people read Richard Lovelace

sea cows trying to pass as manatees

politicians who act like politicians

identity theft

having to convert from kilometers to miles to nautical miles

they shut down Luna Park

the realization that a sou just ain't what it used to be

persons who got no goddamn couth

holes in the ozone layer

holes in the Mohorovicic layer

the invisible hole that turns up in my racket every time I play
    tennis
belief in the divine right of kings
that I never learned to speak Mandarin
people who ride bicycles on the sidewalk
people who come into the theater after the trailers, just as the
    film is starting, and then loudly complain because they
    can't find a seat
ipecac in my Bovril
martinets
bad Chinese food
bad Hungarian food
bad Ethiopian food
bad food
having to put additional holes in my belt
life really isn't a box of chocolates
nor a bowl of cherries
the inevitability of the cable company raising its rates every few
    months
too many schools have paint peeling off classroom walls
the scarcity of billabongs in North America
the G. W. Bush library is reputed to be running out of crayons
nihilism
baleful dreams

the best laid schemes o' mice and men that gang aft a-gley

the little train that couldn't

needing only one last entry to finish the crossword puzzle and
      not knowing the Assyrian word for hockey

soccer hooligans

"Free" offers that end up costing several hundred bucks

e doesn't = mc^3

when call waiting won't wait any more

when my tweeter overpowers my woofer

the nurse who, just before giving me the needle, says, "Take it
      like a man."

a peppermint parfait in a Styrofoam cup

any exam that begins with the prefix procto-

losing an opportunity

losing my composure

losing my keys

losing my hair

cemeteries as tourist sites

when tickets went up to 15 cents a dance

a bassoon in a mariachi band

inane interviewers on TV talk shows

meringue that droops

talentless singers who don't have enough sense to know they
      may be offending their listeners

people who don't like my vocalizing
deceptive advertising
people who have initials instead of a first name
turgid prose
noisy shoes
turgid shoes
noisy prose
glass blown with garlic breath
no matter what time it is anywhere in the world, the clock in
    my kitchen reads 1:40
the worship of Moloch
cod liver oil
tipsters at the race track
forgetting the Maine
the price of a coffee at the airport
getting hit with a pie
chocolate sprinkles in my soup
when my boomerang gets lost
a map with no scale shown
a map with no legend
getting hoist by my own petard
getting hoist by anyone's petard
not knowing what a petard is
an infestation of mollusks

sitting on a thorn

saddle sores

a wet blanket

genus envy

when J. Lo doesn't return my calls

splinters in my lip from my chopstick

congressman allowed to rewrite their remarks before they're
    printed in the Congressional Record

many of the uses for a belaying pin

clogged drains

clogged arteries

ghost stories

carnivorous plants

when my screen saver talks back to me

when my Magic Marker dries out

scam artists who prey on the elderly

traffic lights that don't give you enough time to cross the street

unfunny comic strips

waste of natural resources

their old school tie

condescension

Freudian repression

when my bathroom scale lies to me

when my bathroom scale tells me the truth

buying something at a garage sale only to discover that I had
     sold it at my garage sale three months earlier

when my horse finishes dead last

when the other shoe doesn't drop

gas station attendants don't clean car windows any more

"Ladies?" I thought the sign said "Laddies"

increased productivity (translated to longer work days)

shrinking annual salary increases

shrinking annual salaries

automobiles on which the front end looks exactly like the back
     end

auto protection systems that talk to you: "Please step back. You
     are too close to the car."

authors who write the same book several times

a glass that's half full is also half empty

guns in the hands of children

alligators on the golf course

polo as a college sport

when the people in the next apartment blast their Tiny Tim
     CD at full volume

they should have cancelled New Year's Eve when Guy
     Lombardo died

discovering I'm persona non grata at KFC

history is written by the victors, but it is not always accurate

I can't wear pince-nez

when I stand up my lap disappears

Dali leaving his painting out in the sun until the watch melted

Schopenhauer's lampoon of women as the "unaesthetic sex"

you can't do much with one scissor

Sam Spade never did find the real Maltese falcon

there's no chair lift up Mt. Everest

I can't find anyone who knows the lyrics to Ayers Rock

the woman sitting behind you in the movie who repeats every
    line of dialog from the screen

the half-life of hydrogen peroxide

receiving an overdue notice the day after a payment was due

receiving an overdue notice the same day a payment is due

receiving an overdue notice the day before a payment is due

art museums that don't have even a single Van Gogh

that date who tried to dress me in hot chocolate

the adventures we're missing while we sleep

people who finish your sentences before you do

people who invade my space

people who wear lampshades at parties

people who spend their lives shopping

people who keep pet emus

overnight guests who stay for weeks

the death of planets

what I can't do with a hula hoop

burnout

cold sores

undercooked meatballs

overcooked veggies

destruction of the rain forests

pickpockets in Covent Garden

the pigeon droppings in Piazza San Marco

secondhand smoke

zhang

people who believe that Joshua fit the battle of Geritol

people who tell you how the picture ends before you've seen it

when the neighbor's kids play handball on the side of my house

politicians controlled by the big contributions of wealthy
    special interest groups

when my hard drive is overloaded

where we once had statesmen we now have only politicians

watery grits

soggy bacon

soggy grits

watery bacon

gritty bacon

soggy water

surgeons who drink on the job

dentists who drink on the job

barbers who drink on the job

enemas

signs at government office waiting rooms that say, "Take a
number and have a seat"

when the bulb burns out just as I start the last page of a mystery
novel

how the church treated Tycho Brahe

a whole generation that knew great literature only from the
pages of Classic Comics

the extreme bipartisanship in Congress

the Star Chamber

the McCarthy era

barber shops that will "Cut your hair while you wait"

the authorized edition of the Bible printed in London in 1631
that inadvertently omitted the negative from the seventh
commandment, listing it as "Thou shalt commit adultery."
(It became known as the Wicked Bible.)

no one seems to know when the swallows *leave* Capistrano

the disappearance of the good five-cent cigar

the disappearance of loosies

the disappearance of the Charlotte Russe

the disappearance of Judge Crater

dandelions in my lawn

vole holes in my lawn

rabbits in my cabbage patch

bats in my belfry

animal crackers in my soup

when someone laughs at my beret

when someone doesn't laugh at my jokes

when the fit hits the Shan

wherever you escape to, there you are

when my dentist damages a healthy tooth and then charges for
the dental work to repair it

commentators who talk about "nucular" energy

the stingy tipping habits of the very wealthy

the lack of real purpose or real conviction in our political
leaders

new money posing as old money

finding the toilet seat up in the middle of the night

finding several puddles of water on the sink

when the stars are out, you can see them; when the lights are
out, you can't see anything

getting pulled over for speeding when everyone around me is
going faster

women putting on their makeup while driving

men putting on their makeup while driving

hairy mesomorphs with pigtails and unisyllabic vocabularies

people who wear white after Labor Day

men buying feminine hygiene products with a coupon

calling an 800 number for product information and being transferred to another number,

then being transferred to another number, then to another number . . .

when Newt Gingrich tried to shut down the government because he felt "snubbed" while traveling on the president's plane

newspapers that put the inflammatory charge on page 1 and the subsequent retraction on page 42

people who ask, "Can I ask you a question?" Which they just did.

getting the same e-mail joke from several people

books on management that repeat the same insipid, self-evident observations

loving my government, but not trusting my government

the worst drivers seem to drive the biggest cars

the confusing, unpronounceable names they give to prescription drugs, all meant to intimidate the user and increase the price

holier-than-thou poseurs

smugness

little happy faces

passing the buck

people who won't take responsibility for their actions

boxing is considered a sport even though its intent to render
the opponent unconscious

poaching endangered species

the loosened standards of morality applied to sports stars and
show business figures

sport utility vehicles with ski racks and handicap license plates

people who vie for the parking spot nearest the gym entrance

Boston drivers

twenty-four-hour toll-free hotlines answered by a recording

banks with ten windows and one teller

people I don't even know telling me to have a nice day

banks that want to give me a loan when I have money, but
won't when I have none

American flags made in China

EZ tax forms that come with ten pages of instructions

household cleaner made from real lemon and lemon juice made
from chemicals

doctors who wear $9,000 Rolex watches and still don't know
you've been waiting for an hour

clerks at the health food store who are in worse shape than I am

stale Twinkies

prejudicial jokes

finding the sleeping pill bottle open on my wife's night table
after I've taken my Viagra

buying an oriental carpet at full price

after finishing a dinner at an expensive restaurant and then
finding out they don't have valet parking

unpacking my home computer and realizing there is no
available nine-year-old to assemble it

calling the computer company for help and finding out the
nine-year-old's fourteen-year-old brother is the president

my environmentalist neighbors who have their lawn sprayed
commercially every month

any product that requires assembly

the mental midgets who interview arrivees at awards dinners

the undue adoration we give celebrities

musicals so derivative you walk *into* the theater whistling the
tunes

when the contents of food cans shrink but the cans remain the
same size

I never dined where the elite meet to eat

never getting my fifteen minutes of fame

it wasn't bigger than a breadbox

cracking gum

the reduced attention span of the average American

recycled homilies passing as original ideas

factoids

chatterboxes

reckless golf cart drivers

failing an IQ test

not knowing anyone at a party I'm invited to

people who don't RSVP

little white panties on lamb chops

political campaign literature that lies

ants on my picnic blanket

a 2-cents plain now costs 75 cents

boom boxes

what passes as a college education

newspaper columnists who are always on an ego trip

The Nonadventures of Ozzie and Harriet

sumo has never been made into a musical

Doris Day remained a virgin

graffiti "artists" who pollute the cityscape with their gratuitous
    intrusions

self-destructive clichés like "no pain, no gain"

jingoism

ostentation

affectation

disrespect

malevolence

not fulfilling one's promises

Christmas season starts earlier every year

the professor on Gilligan's Island who could make a microwave
oven out of a banana but couldn't fix a hole in the boat

a Nobel Prize went to Dr. Antonio de Egas Moniz for developing prefrontal lobotomy—the practice of which fell into
disrepute within ten years after the award

Lilliput never played Brobdingnag in the finals

terrorists

leaders who don't lead, but are led by opinion polls

it took almost twenty years for Susan Lucci to win the damn
statue

losing a day crossing the International Date Line

an Australian without his tinnie

politicians who can't keep their pants zippered

karaoke

morganatic marriages

the large number of unnecessary surgeries performed each year

the bumps on my head

people who practice phrenology

soaps that lather up profusely but don't clean anything

colorizing movies

the banality of violence in America

being out of the grid

being out of sync

being out of toilet tissue

credit card interest rates

stock market "corrections"

butter-fingered aerialists

when I fly to London, but my luggage ends up in Katmandu

flotsam

jetsam

General Electric avoiding taxes by moving everything over-
    seas—including jobs

odorized pages in magazines

ocarina bands

the megalomania of Donald Trump

chopped liver sculptures

politicians using lotteries to raise money

when the cable goes dark

rains delays at the ball game

getting a zit on the tip of my nose

toxic waste in my backyard

when driving over a small pothole inflates my air bag

 the political naiveté of the American people

the way we treated Native Americans

people with 20-20 hindsight

not finding a vacant seat on the subway

soft money fueling elections

anyone with an attitude

selling dog doo on the Net (e.g., at crap-o-gram.com)

presidential candidates who promote one platform in the
    South and the opposite in the North

going broke investing in Lloyd's of London

the OPEC oil cartel

kowtowing

the ghost of Christmas present

singers who have no idea what the melody is

what I had thought was a classic is just an old car

bumper stickers that say, "Honk if you're a honkie."

writers with no Sprachgefühl

Little Orphan Annie has no eyes

Peanuts has no hair

Dagwood never got a haircut

Donald Duck wears no pants, he exposes himself but—Donald
    Duck has no genitals

Tarzan never sent his loincloth to the laundry

Rocky XXXIV

Lombroso's theory of criminal behavior

Pat Sajak wouldn't let me buy a vowel

vanity license plates

bad table manners

we left it to Beaver

mother knew that father didn't know best

we ask not what we can do for our country, but what our
country can do for us

politicians don't get indicted for lying to us

unisex lavatories

photos glamorizing teenager Miley Cyrus

high-pressure Amway representatives

pyramid schemes

friends who won't lend me money

mathophobia

mystery novels in which two teenage girls solve the crime and
make the police chief look foolish

Herc never made it with Xena

alarm clocks

solecisms

tyrants

the French Revolutionary judge who sent Antoine Lavoisier to
the guillotine, saying the Republic had no need for
scientists.

taxation without representation

dirty money

money laundering

worshiping Mammon

worshiping Baal

worshiping the buck

sticky wickets

fox hunting

vainglory

forlorn hope

insider trading

outside plumbing

golden parachutes

backbiting

lawyers

politicians

the increasing numbers of children born into fatherless homes

being picked out of a lineup

being asked how much money I make

hearing the order to "abandon ship!"

when the string breaks on my kite

when the string breaks on my yo-yo

when my uncle got a suspended sentence: he was hanged

the taste of canned spaghetti

the idea of canned spaghetti

graphic vomiting scenes in movies

supercilious displays of disdainful pedantry

I want to stop, but inertia won't let me

there are no more celebrities available for guest shots on talk
   shows. They all have their own talk shows.

when I can't make 8 the hard way

when my neighbor's dog howls all night

when my neighbor howls all night

I've reach the age at which my pill case weighs more than my
   clothes bag

"y'know?"

when someone else controls the TV remote

shampoo (I want real poo)

virtually no government contract comes in on budget

the oil industry buying Congress

the gun lobby buying Congress

the pharmaceutical industry buying Congress

you can't tell anymore who owns Congress

clothing with the manufacturer's name prominently displayed
   (I refuse to pay for their product and then provide them
   with free advertising.)

lumpy oatmeal

selling Viagra as an Erector Set

tobacco company executives who continue collecting signifi-
   cant salaries hawking a product that will kill up to one-
   third of its users

we don't know what his name was before he changed it to
    Hideki Irabu

short sheets on a hotel bed

Machiavelli showed them how

political expediency

a Starbucks on every other corner

undecipherable computer operating instructions

homophobia

that guy down the block who knows where to get everything
    wholesale

the shape I'm in

moviegoers who talk back to the screen

when someone with big hair sits down directly in front of me
    in a theater

negative-option book or record clubs

designer sneakers

ending up on the slowest checkout line at the supermarket

when my pen runs out of ink right in the middle of creating a
    brilliant poem

when my pen runs out of ink right in the middle of creating a
    magnificent symphony

when my pen runs out of ink right in the middle a poison pen
    letter

downsizing

outsourcing

the liberal media picking on Sarah Palin just because she's
fatuous

hypercompetitive men who make a pissing contest out of every
encounter with another man

the belief that "I shop, therefore I am"

selling caskets on the Internet

hunters who hunt for the sheer fun of killing

HMOs

friends expecting you to watch videos of their family get-
togethers

people who act without thinking

actors who act without thinking

intellectuals who think without acting

blaming the victim

honi soit qui mal y pense

kindergarten teachers whose vocabulary is exclusively monosyllabic

questionnaires that come in the mail probing my buying
preferences, my sex habits, or my politics

paid "volunteers" who appear at my door soliciting contributions to unknown causes

legislators who are "pro life" but won't finance child health
programs

we keep getting more and more cable channels, and there's still
    nothing worth watching

parents who start sentences with, "When I was your age. . . ."

summer TV reruns

chapped lips

Curtis Sliwa hasn't been appointed New York Police Commis-
    sioner

a black bra under a white blouse

"Do as I say, not as I do."

people who go out constantly because they don't like their own
    company

prison tattoos, especially on women

ATM charges

my microwave picks up the Milton Berle show

bragging

people who kiss and tell

vacation tours that visit twenty-two cities in nine days

New York City cab drivers who route tourists from LaGuardia
    airport to midtown by way of Detroit

the disgraceful Staples stationery stores' school commercial
    that used to appear every August, portraying a father
    ecstatic that his children will be returning to school, while
    they are downright catatonic at the prospect

the opulent lifestyle of some religious leaders

mental implants

extra-sensory deception

the final score of the Yale vs. William and Mary game was Yale
     12, William 6, Mary 3

the nouveau riche

I think it was a negative, but I'm not positive

Santa knows if I've been naughty or nice

being voted Mr. Congeniality in the weight-lifting contest

half the distance to the goal line

Sgt. York never made lieutenant

health enthusiasts who jog ten miles in the health club, then
     take a taxi six blocks to home

$6 + 6 = 14$ in base 8

static cling

exposing the private lives of public figures

dieters who end their low-cal garden salad lunch with a
     chocolate fudge sundae and extra whipped cream

Glenn Beck claiming that his supporters are "the protectors of
     the civil rights movement"

Soupy Sales is gone

erotic dreams about Dr. Ruth

there's no such thing as pain in a hospital, only "discomfort"

recent research that indicates more American students know
     the names of the three stooges than know the three
     branches of American government

when you have to go to the bathroom on an airplane right after
 securing your safety belt

people who never let fact intrude on their opinions

the astronomical cost of popcorn in a movie theater

Little League parents so intent on winning they don't let their
 kids enjoy the game

the Broadway theatre has become so torpid that they're now
 giving Tony awards for the best revivals

Halliburton, the company run by ex-VP Dick Cheney, ripping
 off the US government

not knowing the question to the final Jeopardy answer

souvenir plates with celebrity's faces painted on them

the degradation of the American palate with the blossoming of
 fast-food chain restaurants

mechanized telephone solicitations that begin with, "Please
 hold on for an important call."

someone else's leverage

people who put their dogs in sweaters

the store doesn't take credit cards

the greed of sports teams' owners

the greed of ball players' agents

the women at my beach don't look like the Baywatch babes

Scotty refuses to beam me up

"If you were a tree, which one would you be?"

I can't figure out why glue doesn't stick to the jar

nicks in my windshield wiper blade

of 1,000 US citizens to take the test given newcomers to
    qualify for American citizenship, only 38 percent passed

"the truth of the matter is . . ." (a phrase usually followed by an
    ignorant misperception or an outright lie)

pop-up commercials on my computer

modspeak, such as "so fun"

kids texting in abbreviations

the new packaging that requires the strength of a gorilla to
    open

it's getting tough to find a player piano

my Aunt Jody turned out to be my Uncle Jody

"Made in America" stickers made in China

I've never been invited to dance with the stars

the pointlessness of the necktie in men's clothing

SuperPACs

the 2012 Republican presidential candidates vying with Rush
    Limbaugh to ascertain who among them has the greatest
    disdain for American women

I can't keep up with the renaming of neighborhoods in New
    York City: SoHo, NoHo, NoLita, Dumbo, Bimbo

the Academy Award statue might just as well have been called a
    Felix

bullying

all babies look like Justin Bieber

the waste of Whitney Houston's great voice

political attack ads

the disappearance of spats

organized groups that protest at funerals

the designations Republican and Democrat have outlived their
usefulness. We need more defining political party names
such as Conservative, Moderate and Liberal

when the elevator stops between floors

the waif look

the steroid look

the heroin chic look

my mousy picture in my yearbook

making mountains out of mothballs

we are rapidly becoming a zero-sum nation

politicians

lawyers

SECTION 2:

Impolitic Politicians

Politicians and lawyers piss me off, even more so because many of each are both. The main difference is that lawyers have less need to pontificate, and consequently are less likely to display their ignorance. Politicians, on the other hand, with their desire for the spotlight, are more apt to make fools of themselves publicly, to make imprudent or downright empty-headed remarks. The evidence is legion. The verbal contortions by the second President Bush, for example, are well known, having been collected in several volumes and Web sites. But many others in the political realm have also contributed mightily to the aggregate of quoted absurdity in the public sector.

A problem is introduced, however, by the difficulty in distinguishing between politicians who are dumb and those who are deceitful. Politicians are frequently inept, corrupt, stupid, or venal, or any combination thereof. Within recent memory we've had one vice president who resigned in disgrace after being charged with accepting bribes and evading taxes, and another who couldn't spell *potato*. We've had a governor of Illinois who tried to sell a seat in the US Senate. We've had, in 2011 alone, at least one congressman from each party forced to resign after some violation of the public trust.

"Public service" seems to bring out the worst in people.

No doubt striving for absolution, in a 1982 article in the *New York Times* ex-president Nixon is quoted as saying that as a candidate, "You have to dissemble. . . . There's a lot of hypocrisy and so forth in political life. It's necessary in order to get into office and in order to return to office." Should we not be outraged?

Putting deceit aside, here are some of the worst—or best, if you'd rather—political inanities I've run across, including a few from political commentators not directly in government:

"Verbosity leads to unclear, inarticulate things." —VP-elect Dan Quayle, Nov. 30, 1988

"I think that gay marriage should be between a man and a woman." —California Gov. Arnold Schwarzenegger

"If Lincoln were alive today, he'd roll over in his grave."—former president Gerald Ford

"It has been said by some cynic, maybe it was a former president, 'If you want a friend in Washington, get a dog.' ... But I didn't need that because I have Barbara Bush." —Pres. George H. W. Bush

"We have every kind of mix you can have. I have a black, I have a woman, two Jews and a cripple." —James Watt, Reagan's Interior Secretary, describing the formation of a new commission, Sept. 21, 1983. His office later clarified that Watt was merely describing his "broadly based commission."

"If we do not succeed, then we run the risk of failure." —VP Dan Quayle, at the Phoenix Republican Forum, March 1990

"The only way the Republican Party can hold the White House ... is to nominate a candidate who can win." —Alexander Haig, former Secretary of State

"Ninety percent of the politicians give the other 10 percent a bad reputation." —Henry Kissinger

"I resent your insinuendos." —Mayor Richard J. Daley of Chicago

"This is the worst disaster in California since I was elected." —Edmund G. (Pat) Brown, about an earthquake while he was Governor of California

"When I see a 9/11 family on television, or whatever, I'm just like 'Oh shut up.' I'm so sick if them because they're always complaining." —Dissenter Glenn Beck, Sept. 2005

"The only way we'll ever get a volunteer army is to draft them." —Rep. F. Edward Hebert, Chair of the House Committee on Armed Services

"Eighty percent of air pollution comes not from chimneys and auto exhaust pipes, but from plants and trees." —Presidential candidate Ronald Reagan, 1979

"If God had not intended us to eat animals, how come He made them out of meat?" —Sarah Palin

"We have to pass that (health care) bill so you can find out what is in it." —House Speaker Nanci Pelosi, shortly before the health care reform bill became law, March 9, 2010

"One word sums up probably the responsibility of any vice president. And that one word is 'to be prepared.'" —VP Dan Quayle

"Marriage is not a civil right. You're not black."—Sophist Ann Coulter, to a group of gay conservatives, displaying her ignorance of what the 14th Amendment is about, Sept. 26, 2010

"I think the free-enterprise system is absolutely too important to be left to the voluntary action of the marketplace." — Florida Rep. Richard Kelly

"You can't just let nature run wild."—Gov. Walter Hickle of Alaska, explaining why he wanted state authorities to kill hundreds of wolves

"Life is indeed precious, and I believe the death penalty helps affirm this fact." —Mayor Ed Koch of New York City

"That's part of American greatness, discrimination. Inequality, I think, breeds freedom and gives a man opportunity." —Lester Maddox, former Georgia governor

"Excess carbon dioxide in the atmosphere gets sucked down by the trees and helps the trees grow." —Ron Johnson, Tea Party-backed senatorial candidate in Wisconsin, Aug. 16, 2010

"I believe things are on an irreversible trend toward more freedom and democracy. But that could change." —VP Dan Quayle

"The streets are safe in Philadelphia. It's only the people who make them unsafe." —Frank Rizzo, former police chief and mayor of Philadelphia

"I'm not worried about the deficit. It's big enough to take care of itself." —Pres. Ronald Reagan

"The Middle East is obviously an issue that has plagued the region for centuries." —Pres. Obama, Tampa, FL, Jan. 28, 2010

A continued weapons buildup is "absolutely essential to our hopes for a meaningful arms reduction." —Secretary of State Alexander Haig, speaking to the Foreign Relations Committee

"It's no exaggeration to say the undecideds could go one way or the other." —Presidential candidate George H. W. Bush, during the 1988 presidential campaign

"We're going to have the best educated American people in the world." —VP Dan Quayle

"When more people are thrown out of work, unemployment results." —Pres. Calvin Coolidge

"A zebra doesn't change its spots." —Al Gore, attacking George H. W. Bush during the 1992 presidential campaign

"It's about a socialist, antifamily political movement that encourages women to leave their husbands, kill their children, practice witchcraft, and become lesbians." —Televangelist Pat Robertson, 1988 GOP presidential candidate, on the proposed Equal Rights Amendment

"The only way to reduce the number of nuclear weapons is to use them." —Conservative polemicist Rush Limbaugh

"Things are more like they are now than they have ever been." —former Pres. Gerald Ford

"This bill, if passed, will derail the ship of state." —Stanley Steingut, speaker of the New York State Assembly

"Segregation of the races is proper and the only practical and correct way of life in our states." —Florida judge Harrold Carswell, 1948, a comment that kept him off the Supreme Court when he was nominated by Nixon in 1969

"I was recently on a tour of Latin America, and the only regret I have was that I didn't study Latin so I could converse with those people." —VP Dan Quayle

"We shall reach greater and greater platitudes of achievement." —Mayor Richard J. Daley of Chicago

"It's your state that fired the shot heard round the world. . . . You are the state of Lexington and Concord, you started the battle for liberty right here in your backyard." —Presidential candidate

Michele Bachmann, addressing a New Hampshire audience in March 2011

"I've always thought that underpopulated countries in Africa are vastly underpolluted." —Lawrence Summers, chief economist of the World Bank, explaining why he would favor exporting toxic waste to Third World countries

"We've had no domestic attacks under Bush; we've had one under Obama." —Rudolph Juliani, ex-mayor of New York City, Jan. 8, 2010 (Where was he as mayor on 9/11/2001?)

"What does an actor know about politics?" —Pres. Reagan, annoyed by some comment by Ed Asner

"Those who died, their lives will never be the same again." California Rep. Barbara Boxer, after the San Francisco earthquake

"But obviously, we've got to stand with our North Korean allies." —Sarah Palin, on how she would handle the current hostilities between the two Koreas, radio interview with Glenn Beck, November 23, 2010

"I love California. I practically grew up in Phoenix." —Dan Quayle

"Outside of the killings, Washington has one of the lowest crime rates in the country." —Mayor Marion Barry of Washington, DC

"I think we agree, the past is over." —Presidential candidate George W. Bush, on his meeting with John McCain, May 10, 2000

"Well, I learned a lot. You'd be surprised. They're all individual countries." —Pres. Reagan, on returning from a trip to Latin America

"We know of certain knowledge that he [Osama Bin Laden] is either in Afghanistan, or in some other country, or dead." —former Defense Secretary Donald Rumsfeld

"The loss of life will be irreplaceable." —VP Dan Quayle, in a CNN interview about the San Francisco earthquake

"Where in the Constitution is separation of church and state?"
— Christine O'Donnell, senatorial candidate from Delaware, in debate with her opponent, Oct. 13, 2011

"What right does Congress have to go around making laws just because they deem it necessary?" —Marion Barry, former mayor of Washington, DC

"Drug therapies are replacing a lot of medicines as we used to know it." —Pres. George W. Bush

"Fool me once, shame on you. Fool me twice, shame on you." —Rep. Virginia Fox of North Carolina

"There is no Soviet domination of Eastern Europe." —Pres. Gerald Ford, in a 1976 presidential debate with Jimmy Carter

"Nancy and I are sorry to learn about your illness. Our thoughts and prayers are with you. God bless you." —Ronald Reagan, in a 1990 letter to Augusta Lockridge after she was blinded in the soap opera Santa Barbara. Lockridge is a fictional character.

"Rarely is the question asked, 'Is our children learning?'"
—Presidential candidate George W. Bush, Jan. 11, 2000

All of the quotes above merely confirm what President G. W. Bush once told a Yale graduating class: "To those of you who received honors, awards, and distinctions, I say well done. And to the C students, I say, you too can become president of the United States." *[Prescience?]*

And what are we to make of a press release issued by Florida Senator George Smathers attacking his opponent, incumbent Claude Pepper, in the 1950 senatorial race: "Known all over Washington as a shameless extrovert, [Pepper was] reliably reported to have practiced nepotism with his sister-in-law and has a sister who was once a thespian in Greenwich Village. Worst of all, it is an established fact that Pepper, before his marriage, practiced celibacy."?

In summary, this revelation from Harry Truman: "My choices in life were either to become a piano player in a whore house or a politician, and to tell the truth, there's hardly any difference."

SECTION 3:

Great Denials in History

I'm also pissed off by people who don't accept responsibility for what they say or do. Copping out has become a national sport, in which newsworthy personalities deny what most everyone else knows, or suspects, is true. This is a pursuit favored by politicians, but not infrequently practiced by non-governmental figures, usually after a news story detailing the activity or propensity being denied.

Following are some of the most flagrant:

"I am not a crook." —Pres. Richard Nixon

"I'm not an intellectual." —Pres. Ronald Reagan

"I am not a witch." —Delaware senatorial candidate Christine O'Donnell , having once declared on TV's *Politically Incorrect* that she "had dabbled into witchcraft"

"I am not gay." —Sen. Larry Craig of Idaho

"I am not a homosexual . . . . And I've never been to a prostitute." —TV preacher Jim Bakker

"I am not a bimbo." —Jessica Hahn, she of the sexual encounter with Reverend Jim Bakker, after posing for several pages of Playboy topless photos

"I am not a felon." —Pres. Reagan White House aide Lyn Nofziger, entering a not-guilty plea to charges of illegal lobbying

"I am not a wild man nor a schmuck." —New York Mayor Ed Koch, affirming that he would stay on his diet after his heart attack.

"I am not a communist." —Rev. Billy Graham, defending his report that he'd seen no evidence of religious repression in the USSR

"I am not a wimp." —Adlai Stevenson, Illinois gubernatorial candidate

"I haven't committed a crime. What I did was fail to comply with the law." —Mayor David Dinkins of New York City, in response to accusations that he failed to pay his taxes

"I did not have sexual relations with that woman, Miss Lewinsky." —Pres. Bill Clinton

"I never drink coffee at lunch. I find it keeps me awake for the afternoon." —Pres. Ronald Reagan

"We are not at war with Egypt. We are in armed conflict." —P.M. Sir Anthony Eden, 1956

"He's hiking on the Appalachian Trail," reported the office of South Carolina's governor Mark Sanford while he was visiting his girlfriend in Argentina

"We don't have to worry about endangered species—why, we can't even get rid of the cockroach." —James Watt, Secretary of the Interior in the Reagan administration

"Some reporters said I don't have any vision. I don't see that." —Pres. George W. Bush

"The Lord told me it's none of your business." —Preacher Jimmy Swaggart to his congregation, responding to concerns about his having been stopped for erratic driving by the California Highway Patrol and found with a prostitute in his car

"I have no idea what statement was issued, but I stand by it 100 percent." —Richard Darman, budget director in the George H. W. Bush administration

"I don't know who that baby is." —Sen. John Edwards of North Carolina, in 2008, after having been discovered to father a child outside his marriage

"I did not. . . . I've been hacked. . . . Photos can be manipulated." —New York Congressman Anthony Weiner, denying that he tweeted a lewd photo to a woman in Seattle.

"Apparently, I actually have to commit suicide to convince people I'm not running." —New Jersey Governor Chris Christie, once again denying he is a candidate for the presidency in 2012

Now politicians have perfected an artful variation, the non-denial denial. This deceptive equivocation is meant to sound like a denial but really isn't, allowing the speaker subsequently to change course without being accused of having lied. Such phrases as, "It is in my plan to," or "I cannot conceive of ever wanting to," which sound like a promise to follow a specific course of action, but are ambiguous enough to later lay blame on the listener for misinterpreting rather than on the speaker for misrepresenting.

A recent example comes from Texas governor Rick Perry, who had repeatedly indicated he would not seek the presidency, "under any circumstances." As late as May 2011, he told Greta Van Susteren, "This isn't something that I want to do." (Note this is not a definitive rejection.) Less than three months later he declared his candidacy.

On the other hand, why should we expect our elected officials to give us straight talk? There are really no constraints on them, other than their inherent honesty, which at best is in extremely short supply. If they lie to us (note the conciliatory "if" in place of the more realistic "when"), our only recourse is to vote them out at the next election. But our memories are short, and when election time rolls around we are still stuck with the need to decide which of the candidates has lied to us less. We frequently must choose between the devil we know and the devil we don't.

Nor are the courts any help. Our legal system provides no redress for having been misled by a politician. In New York, in 1912, a voter became angered at a recently elected official who, upon taking office, neglected to fulfill any of the campaign pledges he had made. Having backed the candidate, in support of the candidate's stand on several issues, the voter proceeded to sue him for breach of oral contract, arguing that his vote was given in exchange for the promises made by the candidate during the campaign, a quid pro quo, and thus qualified as a contractual obligation.

The judge disagreed. In a decision that still rankles today, the judge ruled against, noting that a contract "cannot be based on an ante-election promise to voters generally by a candidate for public office, so as to give a voter a right to restrain the promise from violating same." That simply means we can't hold a candidate legally responsible for the lies he tells us when campaigning. Which gives politicians free rein to say whatever they choose to solicit votes without any obligation to fulfill their pledges after they've taken office. (Check it out: O'Reilly v. Mitchell, 85 Misc. 176, 148 N.Y.S. 88 [Sup.Ct. 1914].)

And in this environment we're trying to raise honest, responsible children! How can we not be pissed off?

The Language of Obfuscation

I get angry at the degradation of our language. Few people speak proper English anymore, and many college graduates can't write an intelligible sentence. I seem to remember several years ago some newspaper authority issued a directive to reporters to use simpler expressions in their writing, in other words to contribute to the dumbing down of our discourse.

Words have power, but no longer clear meanings. Things are no longer what they seem. We've moved into a world of euphemisms. Yesterday's poor are today's economically disadvantaged; yesterday's porn star is today's adult entertainer; bald is now follically impaired; the disabled are now physically challenged; slow learners are now special children; what was once a mole is now a beauty mark. This Orwellian verbal camouflage is intended to alter our perception of the world, either to alleviate the unpleasant, enliven the banal, or obscure the unsavory, immoral, or illegal. Which suggests that you actually *can* fool all the people some of the time.

In two books, George Carlin has given numerous examples of euphemisms. Thousands more exist. Here is a choice baker's dozen of the most common.

A device meant to shade the truth, the euphemism is naturally favored by minions of government, by politicians who are adept at subterfuge of one form or another. Not only do politicians lie to us, make inane observations, downright dangerous decisions, and issue denials, on a more conscious level they try to distort the truth by adopting an intentionally misleading language—Governmentese—as though relabeling something changes it. They seem to ignore Shakespeare's admonition, "A rose by any other name. . . . "

What once was:	Is now:
toilet paper	bathroom tissue
phone messages	voice mail
theater	performing arts center
gym	workout center
servants	domestics
complaint department	customer relations department
personnel department	human relations department
homosexual	gay
secretary	administrative assistant
auto dashboard	instrument panel
sales clerk	product service associate
teacher	educator
old people	senior citizens

To wit:

What we have known as:	Is now called:
government inactivity	benign neglect
tax increase	revenue enhancement
the poor	economically disadvantaged individuals
unemployment	underutilization
welfare subsidies	income maintenance programs
a lie	a terminological inexactitude
major disagreement	serious and candid discussion
prison	correctional facility
neutron bomb	enhanced radiation device
nuclear power plant explosion	rapid energy disassembly
acid rain	poorly buffered precipitation
airplane crash	premature impact of an aircraft with terrain
inaction	watchful waiting
military attack	aggressive defense
surprise attack	preemptive strike
killing people	taking action
troop retreat	strategic redeployment

civilians killed in war		collateral damage
bombarding our own troops		friendly fire
overthrow of a foreign government		destabilization (as per the CIA)
official spying		surveillance
assassination		termination with extreme prejudice
insurgents on our side		freedom fighters
insurgents on the other side		revolutionaries, or terrorists
shell-shocked	(to battle fatigue to)	post-traumatic stress disorder
genocide		ethnic cleansing
weapons		military assets
illegal alien		undocumented nonnational
selling public lands		asset management
coffins		crew transfer containers (as per NASA after the Challenger disaster)

It would seem that Rudolf Flesch's charge to *Say What You Mean* no longer applies, as we no longer mean what we say.

SECTION 5:

TV or Not TV

A nother thing that pisses me off is how lame television has become.

TV was once heralded for its dual promise, both as a source of entertainment and as a convenient medium for expanding knowledge, capable of bringing learning directly into the household. But over time, it has not satisfied its potential as an agent of education and is now primarily a provider of diversion.

And likely the prime source of American entertainment—it's watched at home in relative comfort, requires no travel, no entrance or parking fees, and escapes obnoxious strangers locating nearby (excepting the immediate family). But as amusement, TV has become languid, a bastion of slavish imitation, where if it worked once it's sure to work again . . . and again.

It has been said that radio got the family back into the home, but it was television that got them all into the same room. Now, with TV screens that can fill a wall, we have more channels than ever before, and less worth watching. In 1961, Newton Minow, President Kennedy's appointee as chairman of the FCC, called television "a vast wasteland." Minow had no idea how vast it would become or how much waste it would generate.

Here are some of the shows you'll see this season, and every season to come:

Reality TV show: A gaggle of uneducated buffoons move in together and explore the advantages of group living unencumbered by geniality, refinement or simple courtesy.

Four or five women sit around, confer, and project their total misunderstanding of current news events.

Four or five women sit around, confer, and dish other women not on the panel.

Competition show: A number of untalented people from all walks of life perform (sing, dance, juggle, twirl batons) to compete for a coveted chorus role in a new musical opening in Sheboygan, Wisconsin.

The surgical staff at a big city medical center—under a nosy meddlesome boss but with endearing supportive colleagues—play a variety of rib-tickling pranks on their terminal patients.

A single mother trying to balance her professional life—under a nosy meddlesome boss but with endearing supportive coworkers—and her domestic life with a daughter of dangerous dating age and a neighbor she has hots for (or, alternatively, has hots for her).

A dedicated female CIA agent—under a nosy meddlesome boss but with endearing supportive colleagues—who weekly outsmarts her opposite number from an adversary nation, and nightly goes out in search of men.

An ex-cop, who was drummed out in disgrace, confronts the underest of the underworld, devising creative ways to beat them at their own game,

Reality TV show: Cameras follow the members of a remarkably uninteresting family as they go about their boring daily chores: buying groceries, cleaning the grout in the shower, getting the kids off to their violin lessons, having new bushes implanted.

Reality TV show: Cameras follow the members of a remarkably uninteresting family as they go about their boring daily chores: buying diamond necklaces, posing for fashion pics at a polo match, leasing a yacht for their niece's divorce party, having new boobs implanted.

A variation of this show focuses on one celebutramp as she plies her social calendar, offering the viewer not the slightest suggestion of entertainment other than the opportunity to observe her vacuity and narcissism.

Life on a college campus: One dumb jock, one computer nerd, one busty blonde, one pair of interchangeable twins, and an overbearing professor who is repeatedly frustrated by their disobedience and their subversive shenanigans.

Sunday morning sermoner, tending toward prolixity, who preaches the rewards of virtue in a God-centered life, and who in real life is stopped by the police with a prostitute in his car.

A competition show imported from the Far East has contestants perform life-threatening stunts for the chance to appear as a contender on a competition show having contestants perform life-threatening stunts.

A travel maven takes the audience vicariously to exotic locales where they sample local rites, view captivating scenery, and suffer dyspepsia from indigenous vittles.

Sitcom: A couple, she an empty-headed screw-up always plunging into self-induced predicaments, he a compliant twit who is constantly saving her from herself.

Sitcom: A couple, he an empty-headed screw-up always plunging into self-induced predicaments, she a compliant twit who is constantly saving him from himself.

Four or five unfortunately unattractive women are run through a number of rigorous trials to determine who is best suited for success in the modeling world.

A housewifely female, regaled in upswept coif and freshly ironed apron, welcomes viewers into her stage kitchen and leads them through the intricacies of creating attractive but inedible gustatory delights.

Interstellar police fight off evil interlopers from a variety of dark planets in spectacular gravity-free environments.

A failed actress/singer/celebutant sells cheaply made perfume/jewelry/sportswear, under her personal label at severely inflated prices.

The doings of vampires who mistreat other vampires who are mistreating other vampires.

A group of friends in some dangerous public service—firefighting, ocean salvage, in-air balloon repair—every week save the populace from another extremely destructive threat.

Daily afternoon sudzy drama has a group of a dozen or so emotionally insecure characters experiencing unlikely situations and implausible relationships. Cast must include one salacious man, at least one promiscuous woman, a pair of childhood friends now estranged, a deviously controlling wealthy businessman, a woman with no children who wants one, a woman with several children who wants none, and one prodigal child who threatens to but never comes home. Its mirror-image precursor has been on-air since the Eisenhower administration.

Three vacuous girls, skimpily dressed, who share an apartment and their lust for the guy next door.

Three vacuous guys, mostly shirtless, who share an apartment and their lust for the hottie next door.

An afternoon confrontation show to which a sleazy host invites a pair of antagonists to unload on one another, and then provokes the guests into a fistfight.

Members of some performing fraternity get together to congratulate themselves over dinner and award statuettes for some overestimated "artistic" accomplishment.

A squad of cops (at least one a woman) ingeniously solve unsolvable crimes in forty minutes (leaving the other twenty minutes for commercials).

A firm of lawyers who engage in intramural sexual affairs and win hopeless cases by inventive application of obscure laws.

Isolate a half-dozen narcissists in some exotic setting, give them pointless tasks to perform, and see who makes the biggest fool of himself, or herself.

A well-groomed enthusiast, with perfect teeth, predicts tomorrow's weather, sometimes even accurately.

Tort-uous judge who applies a distinctly idiosyncratic interpretation of the law in resolving conflict between pairs of litigious adversaries, making snap decisions in the face of insufficient evidence.

A yenta who delights in revealing the romantic affairs, social gaffes, and arrests of celebrities (several her reported friends).

People posing as reporters, although none has ever journalistically covered a real event, who read the news as though they understand it.

Late-night variety show with a stock format: Monologue, guest interview, house band, guest interview, comedy bit, guest musical group, guest interview, etc. . . .

Reality TV show: the real housewives of East Mayberry, strident harridans who argue, backstab, and unintentionally display how tedious life in East Mayberry really is.

Soft porn: The romantic adventures of three or four women, friends and companions since their parole, all apparently unemployed but residing in upscale apartments and sporting trendy revealing clothes, who seem to be inadequate at everything but buying yet another pair of new shoes.

CSI-Anywhere, boasts the same interchangeable plots in different locales.

Contributed home videos intended to elicit laughs by displaying people doing things tbat will likely land them in the hospital.

Competition show: One guy has to choose a date from among four unappealing women on the basis of their answers to inane questions.

Competition show: One woman has to choose a date from among four unappealing guys on the basis of their answers to inane questions.

Saturday morning staple has an apparently benevolent adult (who secretly disdains children), possibly dressed in brightly colored costume, who leads precocious tykes into parent- pleasing displays of knowledge, character, and neighborliness. During commercials he surreptitiously slips offstage to sample his single-malt and maybe take a toke or two.

Get-rich-quick show, on which contestants—some individual, some whole families—vie for instant wealth in response either to a quiz, a lottery, or a spin of a wheel. The host, with no discernible talent other than a gracious affability, is frequently referred to as "the star of our show."

A hard-sell, fast-talking salesman in the early morning hours loudly hawking specialized kitchen utensiles, "but if you call within the next ten minutes, we'll double the order."

SECTION 6:

Movie Clones

Not unlike TV, the movies seem to be losing their grip on American culture. And on originality. I'm both annoyed and disappointed that film is no longer central to our understanding of the world we live in. No longer do the movies reflect who we are.

Filmmakers once made pictures about people; now too often about contrivances, explosions, and novel cinematic techniques. The price of theater tickets has soared, but as the number of new movies has proliferated, creativity and innovation have eroded. The great filmmakers of the 1930s and '40s have not been replaced. A few working directors do manage to evade banality, but by and large Hollywood has lapsed into an assembly line of clichés.

The industry seems to be governed by creative memories. Whatever the genre, it all looks too familiar.

Here are some of the clones I've seen much too often:

The star gets laryngitis and the understudy has to fill in on the very night the movie scout is in the audience.

Every bomb has a digital clock attached so you know exactly when it is scheduled to explode.

The drill sergeant who was the scourge of his training platoon will stay back to hold off the enemy troops while his men escape from the indefensible position.

The nerd who doesn't drive a car, who borrows clothes from other students, turns out to be the millionaire heir to the moustache wax fortune.

A prostitute can redeem herself if she finds an orphan child who needs nurturing.

The atom bomb test will mutate the local population of garden grubs into giant house-devouring monsters.

No one ever has to go to the toilet.

The court-appointed attorney is a drunk who hasn't won a case in twelve years.

The heroine has been hearing voices; her husband has been trying to drive her crazy to inherit her fortune.

If the sound track has a banjo on it, a man will get raped.

Major America—with guile, organizational skill, and a Brooklyn accent—will easily outsmart the inept German commander of the prisoner-of-war camp.

The PI can't solve the case until he has been shot at several times, beaten up at least twice, and exchanged some sophisticated repartee with the woman in black.

No one in the movies can die without closing his eyes.

Any man with a hangover also needs a shave.

Whatever the film is about, at least two cars must be destroyed.

The reformed gangster, now trying to live a virtuous life, will be drawn back into crime by his ex-cronies.

Every window in Washington, DC, looks out at the Capital Building.

Every window in London looks out at the Big Ben clock-face.

Every window in Paris looks out at the Eiffel Tower.

Every window in San Francisco looks out at the Golden Gate Bridge.

The squad screw-up will eventually save the day by getting lost during the big battle and single-handedly capturing the enemy general.

Little girls who don't want their parents to divorce will find a way to keep them together.

The wagon-master has been wounded by an arrow, and as the Indians start to circle for their final assault we hear the cavalry bugle in the near distance.

Being hit on the head will likely cause loss of memory, which can be recovered only by being hit on the head again.

Having been unsuccessful in all his undertakings, a man makes one last attempt to achieve his life's desire by selling his soul to the devil.

Children who have no irises in their eyes will eventually kill their school principal.

The foppish character is really the leader of the tyrant's opposition.

Kindly old doctor ministers to the health and social relations of a small town, while teaching an aspiring young physician that patients are people, too.

Period piece revealing the Romans (barely distinguishable from the ancient Greeks in film) as conniving empire builders who plot, party, and palaver between spectacles.

One of the hijackers turns out to be a federal agent.

An aspiring dance team breaks up when she gets a Hollywood offer and leaves him. But he makes it big on Broadway while her career sinks, and he eventually takes her back to co-star in his next show.

You know the house is haunted if doorknobs turn by themselves, the doors all squeak, and a man's face suddenly appears in the mirror.

The good guy in a Western town always draws faster than the bad guy.

The murderous racketeer is accompanied to the electric chair by his childhood best friend who has become a priest.

He loves her, but it gets complicated when she falls for his brother.

Anyone suspected of being disloyal to the Nazi cause is followed by a gaunt figure in a dark fedora and a full-length leather coat.

She loves him, but it gets complicated when he falls for her brother.

An explosive device can't be defused until one second before it's about to detonate.

If the adolescent players decide to stage a show, one will have an uncle who owns a Hippodrome.

The town hooker knows the visiting cowboy from an earlier time.

The adopted orphan will turn out to be the real child of the leading lady, who had put him up for adoption when she was destitute in her earlier life.

The French court and its formality, under any King Louis, where the ruling class contends with the English, the lower class, and each other, all the while looking extremely uncomfortable in their finery.

People who sleep in caskets are sure to fly out of the castle every night.

A small-town lawyer from the one-man office will defeat the phalanx of Harvard attorneys who represent the tainted corporate defendant, and will win a large judgment for his client.

She still hates him from the last movie.

A gang of terrorists take over a plane/train/boat and intend to use it to wreck havoc on an American city, but they are foiled by an attendant who, it turns out, is a retired Navy SEAL.

If it's a college musical, there will be an a capella male chorus on the steps of the library singing the school song.

Any scientific laboratory must have equipment producing electrical charges that look like lightning, along with odd-shaped heated glass flasks with bubbles rising to the surface.

Cons will break out of prison disguised as sacks of refuse hidden in the garbage truck.

Incensed at having lost the war, a Confederate squad turns outlaw, raiding towns along the border until finally confronted by a tall loner who grunts one-word sentences.

A hillside Irish town inhabited by lovable old sots and one busty lass is disconcerted by the arrival of a brash American who has inherited the local manor from his great uncle. He is eventually acculturated and taught to wield a shillelagh.

Teen-aged Agnes, who disappears while the family is on vacation in Armenia, will be found and saved by Buster, the family poodle, where she had fallen down a deserted mine shaft.

A New York Lower East Side family has one brother who becomes a gangster while the other joins the police force.

The temptress, who seduces the supermarket bagger to get rid of her husband, will eventually be killed by her lover after she dumps him following the acquittal.

Having learned in the morning that he has just become a father, the bomber pilot will be shot down in that afternoon's mission.

An intricate robbery is accomplished without any problems, but the robbers get caught when one holds out a piece of the stolen jewelry as a gift for his girlfriend.

Depravity and corruption in the upper class is portrayed by the story of the immoral wealthy family living in the mansion contrasted with the virtuous domestic staff living in the small house in back. It is not allegorical.

As the Nazi soldiers are breaking through the door, our heroine resolutely taps out the end of her message exposing the troop locations important to tomorrow's invasion.

Little Jamie, the last player on the bench in the last game of the season, will score the winning touchdown, make the school bully look foolish, and get a kiss from the head cheerleader.

Afterword

So now you know much of what pisses me off. There is more, but I am constrained by decency and the libel laws.

However, what probably raises my wrath more than anything else is the realization that we've become a nation of mindless followers, patsies, conformists. The proverbial different drummer rarely marches anymore. We seem to have an adolescent need to be part of the crowd. We've lost faith in our own critical sense, our ability to judge for ourselves. We're surrounded by hype, and we're so easily conned.

We're conned by unreliable politicians who strive to convince us that what's good for their financiers is good for us. We're conned by mass media restaurant mavens, as we rush off to sample their newest recommended "hot" eatery. We're conned by movie critics not infrequently of questionable taste and lacking substantial knowledge of film history, assigning them authority on what films we should or should not see. We're conned by clothing designers who I fear share a private laugh over our willingness to look foolish in their severely overpriced, up-to-the-minute, often outlandish togs. We're conned by travel writers, who, we suspect, may even be subsidized by travel packagers, inducing us to vacation where the cognoscenti hang out.

In short, we've become a society of lemmings, following the trends, making sure we're "in," but rarely forming our own judgments of what we're doing, or where we're going, or what we're wearing, or indeed what we're thinking—if, indeed, we're thinking at all. It was Samuel Butler who observed that, "The public buys its opinions as it buys its meat or takes its milk." But at what cost?

And if you believe that's worth getting pissed off about . . . you're in the minority, but certainly to be commended.

Reader's List: The Things That Piss Me Off

_____
_____
_____
_____
_____
_____
_____
_____
_____
_____
_____
_____
_____
_____
_____
_____
_____
_____
_____
_____
_____
_____

About the Author

Herb Reich (a.k.a. "him") is a man of many parts, some of which are frequently misplaced. Having essayed several rather checkered careers, his name on formal documents is usually followed by a veritable barrel of manqués. When last gainfully employed, he served as a senior editor with John Wiley & Sons, a highly respected international publisher. The respect accruing to the Wiley company has not rubbed off on him. A few years ago, as the crow flies, he retired from public life to tend his ant farm and grow prize-winning zinnias. Or perhaps tend his zinnias and grow prize-winning ants. His uncertainty is exemplary.

He has also been editorial director of the Macmillan Book Clubs, staff writer at NBC-TV, and an invited contributor to several editions of *The Random House Dictionary of the English Language* and the Corsini *Encyclopedia of Psychology*. (Odd, but true!) He is also the author of *Lies They Teach in School* and *Numberpedia* (both from Skyhorse Publishing).

A rehabilitated onychophagist, he makes his home in Westchester County, where he is now largely unknown and unsung, enjoying the anonymity he so richly deserves. A devout Carmen Miranda fan, he is fanatically color-blind and bats right-handed.

For additional information, consult *Who's Who*.